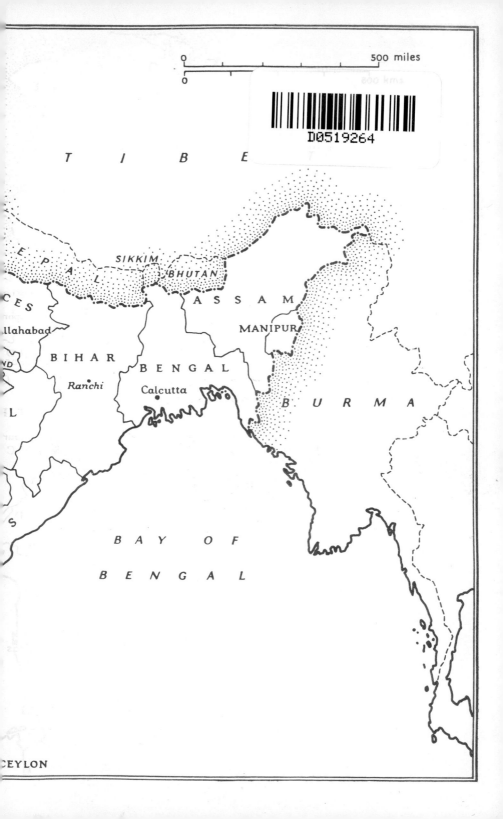

THE INDIA WE LEFT

By the same author

THE MIDDLE EAST IN REVOLUTION
WORLDS APART

THE INDIA WE LEFT

Charles Trevelyan 1826-65
Humphrey Trevelyan 1929-47

HUMPHREY TREVELYAN

MACMILLAN

SBN 333 13426 5

First published 1972 by
MACMILLAN LONDON LIMITED
London and Basingstoke
Associated companies in New York Toronto
Dublin Melbourne Johannesburg and Madras

Printed in Great Britain by
NORTHUMBERLAND PRESS LIMITED
Gateshead

To Susan and Kate who were born there

CONTENTS

6   *Contents*

ILLUSTRATIONS

PREFACE

THIS book is neither a political nor a social history of the British in India, though its underlying theme is the impact of British and Indians on each other in the last hundred and twenty years of British rule. It tells the story of two members of the Trevelyan family, who spent much of their working life in India. The first is the story of Charles Edward Trevelyan, my great-uncle, who went there in the late 1820s for twenty years and, after a period of responsible official life at home, returned to India in mid-century. Secondly, I have written down my memories of what India was like for a young man of the last British generation, who went there a century later and stayed for eighteen years until independence.

These stories are necessarily very different from one another in form and content. Charles Trevelyan's is a very human story of the achievements and failures of a strong, turbulent personality, a complex character with qualities of greatness mixed with rashness, of a man with formidable intellectual powers, unusual energy and immense moral courage, marred by a lack of moderation and humility, who started his Indian career with a fantastic display of determination and independence, rose to the top, fell sensationally and rose again. Throughout it all, he poured out his views on every conceivable Indian subject. Having lived for some time with his papers, I find it difficult not to believe that he is still living round the corner from our house in Wilton Street. When I pass 8, Grosvenor Crescent, where he lived for so long, I find it natural to press the bell and ask if he is at home, which might surprise the ladies of the Red Cross who now occupy it. When I pass the house in Eaton Square where he died, I find it odd not to see the blinds down, the road deep in straw and a row of carriages stopping to allow their occupants, enveloped in deepest mourning, to leave their cards of condolence with the corners turned down. I hope I can communicate a little of that interest to those who meet here for the first time that crabbed, remarkable person, though we can only make up our image of him from his semi-official correspondence, his unending stream of pamphlets, a few family letters and one personal memory of him in old age.

I went to India because Charles Trevelyan had been there. His grandson, George Macaulay Trevelyan, the historian, said to me: 'Why do you not go to India like my grandfather, your great-uncle?' I had had no thought of an Indian career, but replied immediately that I would go, and went. I remember walking back to my Cambridge rooms that summer evening, thinking to myself that I had decided the course of my life, but reflecting that it did not seem different from any other Cambridge summer evening. In India I was never in a position of power; the great events of those days passed over my head. My own story is necessarily much lighter, an attempt to recreate the life we led, the way we looked on our little Indian world, our business and recreations, and it is unashamedly spattered with the gossip and the anecdotes which were part of the substance of that life.

Let me anticipate the critics. The two stories do not fit together. Of course not; how could they? They are about two very different people in different centuries. To me these stories, taken together, with all their incompatibility, throw some light, however faint and indirect, on that strange relationship of two so different peoples, thrown together by the chance of history.

What interest is left in the old British life in India? Perhaps, strangely, more than when we were still there, when, until party politics became involved, a debate on India emptied the House of Commons. The British connection with India was a part of British life for two hundred years. Its literature is vast and mostly forgotten. Why add to it? Perhaps because we were the last of our kind. No Englishman can now know India quite in the way we knew it. Perhaps also because, now that historical myths are growing up and distorting history, it is easier to form a picture of how the British looked on India, and how India looked on the British, through personal stories like these, than from the most scholarly of histories.

Throughout the period covered by this book, 'India' meant the old India, now split into the successor States of India and Pakistan, and 'Indians' meant all the inhabitants of the subcontinent. I have therefore used the names in these senses. 'Anglo-Indian' is used to mean a person of mixed British and Indian descent, not, as the term is sometimes used, for the British in India. The two principal characters in the first half of the book are Sir Charles Trevelyan and Sir Charles Wood. 'Sir Charles' means the former; the latter, without disrespect, is referred to as 'Wood'.

My thanks are due to those who have allowed me to use the correspondence and papers of Charles Trevelyan, Macaulay and Charles Wood, in particular, the trustees of the Trevelyan papers and of the British Museum, the librarian of the India Office Library, the Master and Fellows of Trinity College, Cambridge, the Earl of Halifax and Mrs Lancelot Errington. I am also indebted for helpful suggestions to Mr Percival Spear of Selwyn College, Cambridge, who wrote an account of the Colebrooke case in his *Twilight of the Mughals*; and to Sir Olaf Caroe, who explained to me the facts of the frontier battle of 1863, which are also related in his book *The Pathans*. I have not encumbered the text with notes of the sources used. Apart from my own memories, they are almost entirely the letters of the principal characters in the nineteenth-century story and Charles Trevelyan's pamphlets. In the chapters of background, I have given the principal sources from which I have pilfered to illuminate the scene.

BRITISH AND
INDIANS

W HEN Sir Charles Metcalfe left India in 1835, he received a message from members of the Indian community, praising his regard for equal justice and contempt for abuse, corruption and chicanery. Sir Charles replied by lamenting that a difference in religion and customs should operate to prevent the benefits of social intercourse between the Indian and European communities and the personal intimacy which was the basis of mutual attachment. He regretted that Indians could not share in the amusements of Europeans and that nothing had been devised which would suit the taste of both communities and bring them together more often. He hoped that in time the obstacles to social intercourse between the communities would be removed. The manners and customs of both changed in course of time and they came to have more in common, but it remained true that British and Indians were never close to one another. The Indians were used to conquerors who were not very different from themselves and who had been reared in the same sort of climate and had the same sort of manners and outlook. If they were not quickly expelled, they were assimilated. The British, unlike previous invaders, could not be assimilated and in the end withdrew.

In the early days, the British traders on the coast, having at first had no fixed intention beyond increasing their trade and wealth and securing their position

for that purpose, had acquired dominion with little
effort as a profitable adjunct of commercial exploita-
tion, over a vast country in a state of anarchy caused
by the weakening of Mughal power. Their moral
standards were no better nor worse than the standards
of the Indian potentates with whom they allied themselves and whom they then subdued. The wealth of
the Indies was ransacked to build those elegant mansions which still embellish the English countryside. The
new conquerors spent most of their lives in India,
adopted some Indian ways and showed no desire to
reform Indian customs. The best of them were probably aloof from Indians, but not contemptuous of
them; the worst probably treated the Indians as badly
as the worst of their nineteenth-century successors,
except where they needed Indian help to serve their
own interests.

In the early years of the nineteenth century, men
like Elphinstone, Munro and Malcolm, scholars and
administrators of vision, imagination and integrity,
had done little more than keep the peace, leaving the
Indian administration in Indian hands and, as a British
historian has written, trusting to education to cure the
social practices which disfigured Hindu society. Their
successors, strongly influenced by the evangelical movement, vigorous in reform and less tolerant of Indian
customs, engaged themselves in the suppression of the
Hindu widows' propensity to throw themselves on
their husbands' funeral pyres and of female infanticide,
that early form of birth control, being imbued with
the idea that they were, in Macaulay's phrase, undertaking the 'reconstruction of a decomposed society'.

English manners and standards changed; the British
nabobs became an extinct species. Dominion brought
a new sense of British responsibility; England became
more involved in India; more British went to India
and retained within their community their British
habits of life. Indian customs and thought could not

have been more different from the background of the
English country-house and rectory from which the new
administrators were largely drawn. They were conscious of being conquerors; with the acquisition of final
dominion and the pacification of the whole country,
there grew up a new barrier between the races, now
rulers and ruled. The new generation had the strength
of superb confidence in being in the right. They were
sustained by their strong faith in the absolute truth
of the Christian doctrine and by the belief that the
British had been selected by God to rule the many
millions of Indian heathen and perhaps even bring
them to the true faith. This spiritual arrogance of a
Christian elect produced men of formidable qualities,
in particular the great figures engaged in the pacification of the Punjab, who gave their lives to their task in
absolute selflessness, but lacked charity and tolerance.

The horrors of the Mutiny for which both sides were
responsible, made relations between the British and
Indian communities more difficult, though many good
men strove to undo the harm caused by that terrible
year. The British, buttressed by their family life, now
that many more British women came to India, became
more aloof. In 1882 Sir Richard Temple wrote that
the root cause of the general tendency to treat Indians
with contempt and the want of good feeling on their
part towards officials, was that there was no real communication between the governors and the governed,
no living together or near one another, as had always
been the custom of Mohammedans in countries which
had been subjected to their rule.

At this time, relations between British and Indians
went through a particularly bad phase as a result of
the planters' agitation against the Ilbert bill, under
which Indian magistrates were to try cases against
Europeans in the districts. The Lieutenant Governor
of Bengal described it as a fierce and perilous conflict
of races, and as having destroyed many years' work

towards mutual regard and toleration. The civil servants always had a warm, fatherly feeling for the Indian peasant who looked to them for protection and his basic needs, but most of them did not get on well with educated Indians and had little sympathy for the stirrings of Indian nationalism. At the time of Curzon's appointment as Viceroy, Queen Victoria commented on their overbearing behaviour towards Indians and Lord Salisbury observed that as the British became more contemptuous, the Indians were becoming more sensitive.

The last years of British rule were disturbed by the inevitable pains of political conflict arising from the British reforms and the concurrent Indian independence movement, though personal relations became closer and more friendly with the acquisition of power and responsibility by Indians in Government and commerce, and the loss of imperial confidence in the future. In spite of the conflict, human relationships were becoming more natural. The Indian struggle for independence was not of great historical significance, though no one realised this at the time. The British were bound to leave India in the mid-twentieth century in any case, since the world balance of power was radically changing. Gandhi's movement accelerated the British departure by some years, but if things had gone a little more easily, it might have been possible for the British to leave India in unity.

British and Indians started from fundamentally different points of view on the quality of British rule in India. Let me put the British side first. Lord Dufferin, Viceroy in the 1880s, wrote that there was no service like the Indian Civil Service in the world, for integrity, courage, right judgement, disinterested devotion to duty, endurance, open-heartedness and, at the same time, loyalty to one another and their chiefs; its members were, to his knowledge, superior to any other class of Englishman. They were absolutely free from any taint of venality or corruption. Curzon wrote that he was magnificently served and that the whole spirit of service in India was different from what it was in England, though in another mood he remarked that he found it a melancholy and inscrutable thing that the Service, the proudest and the most honourable in the world, turned out from time to time some of the meanest and most malignant types of disappointed humanity whom it had been his fortune to meet. But in the matter of race relations, his main combat was with the army.

Whatever their deficiencies in behaviour, most British officials genuinely felt that they were engaged in service to India. It was the 'India we served', to quote the title of the memoirs of Sir Walter Lawrence, Curzon's private secretary. In the eighties, Sir George Grierson had written that each in his own way – administrators, soldiers, scholars, teachers, doctors – had done their best to answer the question how they could help India, and whatever the differences in their abilities and in the nature of their service, had shown a spirit of devotion to duty and of sympathy with the millions among whom their lot was cast. Of course, they did not all live up to Grierson's standard, but there was something in the atmosphere and conditions of life that made people think and act in that mould, however narrow their outlook in many ways. In each generation some must have shared the doubts of Alfred Lyall:

> Has he learned how thy honours are rated?
> Has he cast his accounts in thy school?
> With the sweets of authority sated,
> Would he give up his throne to be cool?
> Doth he curse oriental romancing
> And wish he had toiled all his day
> At the bar, or the banks, or financing,
> And got damned in a common-place way?

But, perforce, nearly all of them stayed and cultivated a sense of service, if only because their life in India would have been pointless without it.

Throughout the last century, serious-minded Englishmen serving in India were concerned to find a moral justification for their presence as conquerors. By the end of the century, the belief of the mid-Victorians that they had come to India to serve the divine will, took on the more secular tone of Curzon's speeches. In a public speech in Bombay he said: 'If I thought it were all for nothing, and that you and I, Englishmen and Scotchmen and Irishmen in this country, were simply writing inscriptions on the sand to be washed out by the next tide; if I felt that we were not working here for the good of India in obedience to a higher law and a nobler aim, then I would see the link that holds England and India together severed without a sigh. But it is because I believe in the future of this country and the capacity of our own race to guide it to goals that it has never hitherto attained, that I keep courage and press forward.' Perhaps his inner feelings were more truly expressed in his words, 'Since men do not know why they exist or whither they go, the only purpose of life must be to do good. Where could that better be accomplished than in India?'

There was another view. Nehru wrote his *Discovery of India* from a British gaol in 1944; so it is not surprising that he should have written with a strong emotional bias. Indeed, he recognised this himself in his remark that the history of the British period was so connected with the happenings of the moment that the passions and prejudices of that day powerfully influenced its interpretation, and that Englishmen and Indians were both likely to err, though their errors would lie in opposite directions. With some of what he wrote, Englishmen would agree; that the coming of the British to India, for instance, brought two very different races together, but that they seldom ap-

proached each other. Perhaps we should also not dispute very strongly Nehru's observation that the
English were a sensitive people, yet, when they went
to foreign countries, there was a strange lack of awareness about them and that in India, where the relation
of ruler and ruled made mutual understanding difficult, this lack of awareness was peculiarly evident.

Nehru owed so much to English thought and traditions that he had to rationalise his intellectual difficulty
by an over-simple division between two Englands, 'the
England of Shakespeare and Milton, of noble speech
and writing and brave deeds, of political revolution
and the struggle for freedom', and the England of the
savage penal code and brutal behaviour, of entrenched
feudalism and reaction, the latter playing the dominant
rôle in India. To Nehru there was a close connection
between the length of British rule in the different
provinces and the poverty which he claimed had grown
during the British period. He attacked British policy
for having deliberately created divisions among
Indians, consistently opposed political and social
change, vehemently resisted Indian education, and
basing their theory of Government on racialism, the
idea of a master-race. All the problems of the day were
a direct result of that policy, the minorities, the lack
of industry, the neglect of agriculture, social backward-
ness and, above all, the tragic poverty of the people.
All this was, to say the least of it, wildly overdrawn.
No one, for instance, who knew the Indian countryside, could seriously claim that the British had
neglected agriculture. We simply cannot accept that
all the social and economic problems of India were
entirely the result of British policy and in no way a
reflection of Indian conditions.

To Nehru, the Indian Civil Service was the world's
most tenacious Trade Union, and its members based
their policy on the principle that anything that was
harmful to their interests must of necessity be injurious

to India. In the land of caste they had built up a caste which was rigid and exclusive. They had developed something in the nature of a religious faith in their own paramount importance, and an appropriate mythology which helped to maintain it, a powerful combination of faith and vested interests, any challenge to which aroused the deepest passions and fierce indignation. Since the Viceroys belonged to the possessing and ruling class in England, they had no difficulty in accepting the prevailing outlook of the Indian Civil Service. They spoke from a noble and unattainable height, secure not only in the conviction that what they said and did was right, but that it would have to be accepted as right, whatever lesser mortals might imagine, for theirs was the power and the glory. 'Generation after generation and year after year, India as a nation and Indians as individuals were subjected to insult, humiliation and contemptuous treatment.' Indians were told that the English were an imperial race, with the God-given right to keep them in subjection. There were two worlds, the world of British officials and the world of India's millions, and there was nothing in common between them except a common dislike for each other.

The truth lies somewhere between these conflicting judgements. Was the Indian Mutiny a sepoy revolt supported by reactionary potentates who wanted to regain their old position and peasants inflamed by rumours that the British Raj was over and by the prospects of loot, or the first Indian war of independence, as it is now officially called in India? Were the British members of the Indian Civil Service a body of high-minded men devoted to the service of the Indian people, or an exclusive caste carrying out a racialist policy and deliberately standing in the way of India's political, social and economic progress? Edward Thompson wrote a little book about the Mutiny, not wholly impartial, called *The Other Side Of The*

Medal. We should not depreciate the face of the medal. For generations men went out from these islands to rule India, most of good, average quality, some of outstanding character, some prejudiced and narrow, a fair cross-section of the British at home. They have given much to India, the English liberal traditions of politics, law and freedom of speech, which still have a profound influence on Indian life, a sound administration and more economic development than Indian politicians are prepared to admit. It is for the successor Governments, beset by insoluble political and economic problems, bitterly hostile to each other, to decide whether they will maintain the good that they inherited, or throw it away for political advantage or from a sentimental conviction that all that the British did must have been bad.

I am far from decrying the achievements and personal sacrifices of the British in India and am proud to have belonged to a great service, as are its Indian members, who, since independence, have borne the heat of the day. But we should also not ignore the other side of the medal, the racial arrogance, the exclusiveness and the lack of understanding and imagination which have sometimes accompanied the British virtues of hard work, efficiency and justice. Perhaps if the British had been less aloof, they would have been less honest and less fair. One cannot have it both ways. We must see both sides of the medal, if we are to form a fair idea of how the British system and social habits developed during that strange, improbable association of a small island off the north-west coast of Europe with a great country of Asia, which influenced both so deeply while it lasted and which will become progressively more difficult to picture, now that the British Empire is one with Nineveh and Tyre and Britain is again a European State.

CHARLES EDWARD TREVELYAN 1826-65

I

THE BACKGROUND AT HOME

CHARLES EDWARD TREVELYAN, an elder
brother of my grandfather, was born in 1807 in the
rectory of Nettlecombe in the Quantocks, a mile up
the valley from the Trevelyans' Tudor country house.
His father, the Rev. George Trevelyan, sometime Arch-
deacon of Taunton, occupied the family living as the
younger son of the baronet, the head of the family.
The Trevelyans had been settled at a place of that
name near Fowey in South Cornwall at least by the
reign of Henry III and had spread over Cornwall and
the neighbouring counties. In the later years of the
Wars of the Roses they had acquired by marriage the
property of the elder branch of the Raleigh family,
which brought them Nettlecombe. In the course of
the centuries they had only occasionally dabbled in
politics, though they had been in trouble during the
Commonwealth from their royalist activities. They had
shown no ambitions towards the great positions of
church and state. George Macaulay Trevelyan wrote:

> Generation after generation went by, and neither
> the world of politics nor the world of letters heard
> talk of the Trevelyans. For five hundred years and
> more they went on, from father to son, pursuing the
> quiet life of country gentlemen in the remote south-

west, farming, collecting rents and taking game, surviving in their middle station the storms that were
sweeping away the great families, as the brushwood
survives when the oak is rooted up.

The parson's son was a favourite with his grandfather, old Sir John up at the big house, who allowed
his grandson to 'sport over the manor', armed, as
George Macaulay Trevelyan writes, 'with an old flint-
lock that would better have served a tall Grenadier at
Minden'. In 1820 he was sent to Charterhouse where the
education seems to have been sketchy, judging by
Macaulay's later comment that his education, like that
of other Indian servants, had been 'huddled up hastily
at home' and that he knew not a word of French. He
already showed the toughness with which he was
endowed, for in December of that year when he was
to go home for the holidays, he was prepared to walk
home from Bridgwater, a distance of about eighteen
miles, in order to save the family expense.

In January 1824 he petitioned the East India Company that they would be pleased to place him in the
East India College in order that, if his behaviour and
attainments should prove satisfactory to the Honourable Court, he might be appointed a writer on the
Madras Establishment. Getting into the college at
Haileybury was a plain competition of influence. His
father was worried that Charles's cousin Willoughby
might be preferred to his son. Willoughby, he wrote,
was not very bright and should be provided as a clergy-
man or in such other profession as he wished. Besides,
he had a liver and should not go to India. The practical question was how to get a large family of sons
settled in the army, the Church or India. The Venerable George need not have been concerned. Charles
was given his appointment to Haileybury and there
passed his Hindi and Persian examinations with such
speed that Lord Combermere recorded his achievement

as being 'no less surprising than it was without an example in the annals of the college'. Perhaps in consequence of his outstanding record at Haileybury, he was transferred to the Bengal Civil Service, where he would have greater professional opportunities than in Madras. Having been refused permission by the Company to make his way to India through Persia and Baluchistan, he arrived in Bombay by sea in June 1826, contented himself with riding from Bombay to Madras and reached Calcutta in October.

He passed his final examination in Calcutta with two gold medals and an official 'eulogium' in the *Gazette*, and in January 1827 was appointed to a junior post in Delhi under the famous Sir Charles Metcalfe, whom every young civilian wished to serve and whom throughout his life he regarded as one of the great men of that time in India. He wrote to his grandfather from Delhi that Calcutta was a very fascinating place and that on that account he had used his utmost endeavours to leave it as soon as possible. It was very much in character. Unfortunately for him, within a few months Sir Charles Metcalfe left the post of Resident in Delhi and was succeeded by Sir Edward Colebrooke, a member of a distinguished 'Indian' family, who had been forty-nine years in the company's service. Towards the end of the year, Lady Amherst, the Governor-General's wife, wrote to a friend that Lord Amherst had been able to appoint the young man to the very situation he had been so long wishing for and for which he was so eminently qualified, that of assistant to the Resident in Delhi, Sir Edward Colebrooke, who had written to thank Lord Amherst for having given him so able an assistant. Sir Edward did not know that he had caught a tartar.

2

THE BACKGROUND IN INDIA

WHAT sort of life was Charles Trevelyan going into, as that precocious young scholar, bristling with ideals, embarked on the long sea journey, which might take him four or five months in those days? Perhaps his family had acquired the collection of aquatints by Charles D'Oyley, son of Hastings's old friend, depicting the life of the European in India, with explanatory text by Captain Thomas Williamson, published thirteen years before Charles made his voyage. The family, anxious about his health in the Indian heat, would on the whole have been reassured. They would have learned that if he was moderate in his habits, he might live as long in Calcutta as in any part of the world. He must take a few glasses of claret with his meals, a little madeira, port only as a tonic after dysentery. He must above all avoid spirits, remembering that in a warm climate 'people are subject to great drought, and one glass follows the other but too rapidly. Various complaints very soon announce themselves, when the inconsiderate tippler speedily passes through the various stages of disease, avoided by society, and his demise is scarcely noticed but by those who are benefited by the vacancy.'

It is surprising that patients survived the treatment given to a patient with a high fever. In one case in

1828 we read that medicine was of no avail. There was a long debate whether the treatment was to be the lancet or a bottle of claret a day. The argument was settled in favour of a diet exclusively of claret and strawberries, after several weeks of which the patient miraculously recovered. He would probably not have recovered from the lancet. For all Captain Williamson's optimism, health was still precarious in those days. In 1823 a lady in Calcutta wrote: 'Here people die one day and are buried the next, their furniture sold the third, and they are forgotten the fourth. O Lord, preserve my husband to me!' Five years later, both she and her husband were dead.

In the early years of the century, there were still few Englishwomen outside the presidency towns of Calcutta, Madras and Bombay. The ladies of country-house or rectory could read about the consequences for the young military officer in his cantonment in terms considered suitable for the English gentlefolk of Jane Austen's generation. The young soldiers, they were told, found matrimony very expensive, and early in their career attached themselves to the women of the country, who accompanied the camps and presented their keepers with numerous progeny. These connections were not, however, 'made by choice, to the neglect of our fair countrywomen'. They were the result of necessity.

The ladies of country-house or rectory can hardly have been reassured by this explanation of the life awaiting their sons and brothers who had been provided with an Indian cadetship or military commission, though it does not appear that this aspect of British life in India in any way diminished their efforts to procure an Indian appointment for the younger sons of the family. But the Venerable George doubtless had no qualms about young Charles, whose tastes do not seem to have lain in this direction. As time went on and more English women came to India, manners changed, though it is recorded that as late as the mid-century it was considered in an officers' mess up country that their colonel had no right to stop one of his officers from appearing at the band parade with his Indian mistress.

Oriental ways of life survived here and there at least until the 1830s. According to Victor Jacquemont, the French botanist, whose letters give a lively description of his travels in North India, William Fraser, the Commissioner of Delhi, with whom Jacquemont became very friendly, lived in an immense Gothic fortress, built by himself at great expense. He kept six or seven legitimate wives who lived together some distance away from Delhi, and had a large number of children, who were all Moslems or Hindus according to the faith of their mammas. When the Governor-General, Lord Auckland, was in Gwalior in the late thirties, his sister, Emily Eden, recorded that they dined with a Colonel J—, who lived 'quite in the native style, with a few black Mrs J—s gracing the domestic circle', when the Governor-General was not there.

Calcutta society was very different. Jacquemont, with the scientist's interest in tribal marriage customs, recorded that portionless girls who had not succeeded in getting married in England, arrived in Calcutta in cargoes for sale (on honourable terms) to the young civil and military officers sent out to govern a territory equal to several French 'Departments', who selected their wives from the society of Calcutta, as they would a girl in the street. It was the British form of female infanticide in those days when the girls who found husbands, would probably stay in India until they were forgotten or dead. Calcutta society had become very respectable and much duller than in the days when William Hickey's dear Jemdanee had been on such good terms with all his friends. Everyone was domestic in their habits. The men worked all day and drove with their wives in the evening, always in the same carriage, and it was considered very bad form for a husband or wife to go to an evening party without the other.

Miss Eden, a very superior person who never settled down in India and always longed for her English home, soon decided that she was not very fond of Englishmen out of their own country, and found Anglo-Indian society decidedly limited. The women read no new books, took not the slightest interest in home politics and reduced every topic to the purely local. Female intellect, she wrote, did not flourish in India. There was a strong confederacy against allowing them to have any ideas and they had ceased struggling against it. She made no allowances for the inevitable effect of living for many years away from England. She found dinner parties at Government House not at all lively. After dinner, all the ladies sat in a complete circle round the room and the gentlemen stood at the further end of it. 'They would probably not have had anything to say if they had met, but it would look better. Luckily it did not last long.' However, it seems that she did not make the most of her intellectual opportunities, for she recorded that Mr Macaulay came to her share at dinner, but found no comment to make in her letter upon his conversation.

The letters of the period give the impression that there was virtually no social contact in Calcutta between British and Indians. The intelligent Englishmen with a public conscience spent their time and energy on 'schemes for the improvement of the natives'; but the Indians were treated as something apart, as objects of purely British benevolence, not as people who might be accepted as an integral part of what we would now call a multi-racial society. That would have been considered to be against the natural order of things.

Of course, the obstacles to social contact between British and Indians were erected by both sides. I have already quoted Sir Charles Metcalfe's view of the basic reasons for the social separation of the two communities.

It would be unfair to judge the British of the time by the standards of independent India, when Europeans and Indians mix in the clubs and their homes. But there was another class of English which regarded the Indians as a lower species, who admitted to beating their servants and who, according to the Chief Justice of Miss Eden's time, when acting as members of a jury, invariably acquitted Englishmen accused of murdering Indians.

The situation was different up country, where there were still the independent Sikhs and the autonomous Rajput rulers who had to be treated on a basis of equality, though social intercourse was somewhat constrained from the differences in manners and customs. We have a picture of Miss Eden trying to insert herself into her brother's conversation with a Sikh grandee, who obviously did not relish having to talk to a woman and was 'sublimely unconscious of what a superior article an Englishwoman was'. Relations with the Raja of Jammu were conducted against a background of horrific stories going round the British camp of dissident subjects being flayed alive, of the number of people without noses and ears and of female infanticide caused by the impossibility of marrying the daughters of the family to anyone lower in the social scale. Miss Eden, a stout feminist, commented: 'I wonder the wives do not get up a little rebellion of their own.'

The country was gradually becoming pacified. Military escorts were used where prudence required it, but over large tracts of the country travel by palanquin seems to have been easy and safe. Miss Eden recorded how a palanquin was brought to her informant's house in the country, containing three little English children, a girl nine years old and two smaller brothers. They were going up to Missouri, had been travelling for three days and had about a week's journey ahead of them. They had not even their names on a piece of paper or a note to the magistrates of the district, but were passed on from one set of bearers to another. They arrived safely in Missouri. It was a tribute to the trustworthiness of the unprivileged Indian.

The British had only recently started to live in Simla. Miss Eden's account of Annandale and rides round Jakko and dances and amateur theatricals has a familiar ring to those who used to spend the summer there a hundred years later.

Twenty years ago [she wrote] no European had ever been here, and there we were, with the band playing the 'Puritani' and 'Masaniello', and eating salmon from Scotland and sardines from the Mediterranean, and observing that St Cloup's 'potage à la Julienne' was perhaps better than his other soups, and that some of the ladies' sleeves were too tight according to the overland fashions for March – and all this in the face of those high hills, some of which have remained untrodden since the creation.

Every Englishman who has experienced the delicious change from the heat of the plains to the cool of the Indian hills will echo her feelings as she reached Simla for the first time:

Now I come back to the air again, I remember all about it. It is a cool sort of stuff, refreshing, sweet and apparently pleasant to the lungs. There never was such delicious weather, just like Mr Wodehouse's gruel, cool but not too cool, and there is an English cuckoo talking English – at least he is trying, but he evidently left England as a cadet, with his education incomplete, for he cannot get further than cuck ...

In the south, Ootacamund in the Nilgiri hills, discovered by the Portuguese in the seventeenth century

and forgotten again, was rediscovered by the British
in the first two decades of the nineteenth century and
was quickly developed as a health resort from the plains.
Macaulay was there in 1834, having travelled all the
way from Madras, as he put it, on men's shoulders. He
described the scenery as the vegetation of Windsor
forest or Blenheim, spread over the mountains of Cum-
berland, and the 'station' as having very much the look
of an English watering place. It was not a very happy
visit. It was during the monsoon and for the first
and last time in his life Macaulay was bored, being
prevented from going for a walk by floods of rain.
There were no books in the place except what Macaulay
had brought with him, among which was *Clarissa Harlowe*. He told Thackeray how he had lent it round
the station until the whole place was in a passion of
excitement about Miss Harlowe and her misfortunes
and the scoundrelly Lovelace. But although Macaulay
did not enjoy himself, the place flourished, soon acquiring that badge of having arrived as a hill station, a
circulating library.

Sport occupied much of the energies of the British
up country, as it always has since Jacquemont gave an
account of an expedition after wild boar and tiger, in
company with young Charles Trevelyan. He did not
consider it a very dangerous sport, since he had found
out that no English hunter had been eaten since Mr
Hastings's day, though falls from a horse came immediately after chronic hepatitis and cholera in the
scale of death in India and the sportsmen therefore
always took a surgeon with them. The hunter was
perched, like a witness in an English court of justice,
in Jacquemont's phrase, in a strong and lofty box,
fastened upon the animal's back, and had with him a
couple of carbines and a brace of pistols.

It sometimes happens [he wrote] that the tiger, when
brought to bay, leaps on the elephant's head, but

that does not concern us; it is the affair of the conductor (mahout), who is paid twenty-five francs a month to run the risk of such accidents. In case of death, the latter has at least the satisfaction of a complete revenge, for the elephant does not play the clarinet unconcernedly with his trunk, when he feels he has a tiger for his headdress; he does his best, and the hunter assists him with a ball point blank. The mahout, you see, is a sort of responsible editor. Another poor devil is behind you, whose duty it is to carry a parasol over your head. His condition is still worse than that of the mahout. When the elephant is frightened and flies from the tiger, which charges him and springs upon his back, the true employment of this man is to be eaten in the gentleman's place.

You can see it all in Edward Orme's prints of Indian tiger shoots. Jacquemont's final conclusion was that India was the utopia of the upper classes. In Europe the difference was between governed and governors, in India between the carried and the carrying, which was much clearer. That observation suits well enough to sum up the society which the earnest youth from Somerset was entering, a society with standards and outlook far removed from the ideas which he had imbibed in his father's parsonage at home.

3

THE PURGE OF DELHI

Fifty years before, William Hickey's friend, Bob
Pott, had paid exorbitantly for the Residency at Mur-
shidabad, a post which Hickey described as the most
lucrative in the Company's service, since the Nawab's
stipend, provided by the Company, passed through the
Resident's hands, 'in which channel a considerable portion of it always stuck to his fingers', and the Resident
acted as purchasing agent for all European articles
bought for the Nawab and, in addition, held an
'advantageous post' as Collector of Customs. But the
changes in public opinion in England and Cornwallis's
reforms had swept away the heights of corruption and
only the remnants of the old habits remained, though
they could still be profitable. Complete financial
integrity, now demanded by the new climate of opinion
at the top, had not yet been fully established.

On the arrival of Sir Edward Colebrooke as Resident
in Delhi, young Charles Trevelyan, aged twenty, newly
appointed assistant to the Resident, became a member
of his official 'family', taking his meals in the Residency
in accordance with custom. He was full of zeal and
never a man to take things easily or compromise with
his demanding conscience. He soon found out that Sir
Edward Colebrooke, his wife and his son were all
engaged in making money on the side.

By old custom, ceremonial gifts in cash or kind were presented to the Resident on the occasion of formal visits. The Resident was supposed to hand them over to the Treasury and could buy articles back, if he wanted to, at a fair valuation. Colebrooke did not hand them over, but took half the cash and handed the other half to the people in the game with him. They saw to it that gifts in kind which went to the Treasury were given a very low valuation, if Colebrooke wanted them. Lady Colebrooke also took presents for herself. When the Resident went on tour, the Chiefs through whose territory he passed had to pay him entertainment money. He took bribes by the device of arranging fake sales of Residency property. He sold the Residency carriage and horses to two Rulers successively, but continued to use them himself. He bought Sir Charles Metcalfe's furniture, never paid him for it, and sold it to a Nawab who had no use for it and never saw it. This was risky, since Sir Charles Metcalfe was now a great man in Calcutta and his younger brother Thomas was one of the Delhi magistrates. Lady Colebrooke and their son operated on their own behalf. She got money from fake sales of jewellery or bought jewellery at nominal prices, while the son took what he could get as presents or nominal loans. In less than two years Colebrooke had sent to Calcutta two hundred thousand rupees over his official salary.

Trevelyan remonstrated, but was told that this sort of thing was always done. He tried to get posted elsewhere, but was refused. So he withdrew himself from the Residency and a period of armed neutrality ensued. Politics became involved, since the Resident's agent, who in the circumstances, could do more or less what he liked, forged the Resident's signature on a document giving assurances to the old rebel, Appa Sahib, ex-Raja of Nagpur, who promptly came out of hiding and started collecting new followers. At this point Trevelyan, with great courage, acted. The weight of local opinion was against him and he could not be certain of the attitude of the authorities in Calcutta. He started proceedings against the Resident's agent in the Delhi Courts. The Resident ordered the proceedings to be stopped on the ground that Charles had no official authority to start them. Trevelyan replied by claiming the right to prosecute as a private citizen. The Resident retaliated by arresting Trevelyan's agent, prosecuting him and ordering his trial to take precedence over the case against his own agent. Thomas Metcalfe, the magistrate concerned, found that there was no case against Trevelyan's agent, but was ordered to commit him for trial. The case went on and the Resident declared that he would have the man taken through the city with his face blackened and mounted backwards on a donkey.

It was an extraordinary battle between the elderly Resident and his young subordinate. Trevelyan pursued his private investigations into the Colebrooke family's misdeeds, while he and Colebrooke exchanged acrimonious notes. Colebrooke wrote that he was not 'out of the coach' yet and demanded to know what was happening in Trevelyan's secret inquiry in which he was going so far as to examine witnesses. Trevelyan replied that he took full responsibility for it and would soon lay the papers before the Resident, who could then judge whether his conduct had been proper. Colebrooke retorted that Trevelyan was making him look ridiculous, as everyone knew that the inquiry was directed against him. The Residency servants were laughing at him and he would not put up with it any longer. Trevelyan replied stiffly that he was only doing his duty, that he had made over the depositions to the criminal court and had forwarded copies to the Government. This was a shrewd blow, which left Colebrooke without an effective retort.

Colebrooke next tried to move Trevelyan out of Delhi to a new job, which Trevelyan described as being

like being sent to Siberia by the Emperor of Russia.
At this point he had a stroke of luck. He fell off his
horse and, before he was fit enough to travel, the
Government of India ordered him to stay in Delhi and
carry on with his inquiries. Colebrooke then started
criminal proceedings against him in the Supreme Court
at Calcutta and did his best to blacken his name with
the officials round Delhi. Meanwhile, Trevelyan had
taken the final step. He wrote to the Chief Secretary
in Calcutta charging Colebrooke with corruption, asking for an investigation by two or more officers and
stipulating that it should not be conducted by Jacquemont's old friend, William Fraser, the Commissioner,
who was one of Colebrooke's strongest supporters. In
view of the rate at which Fraser had been living in
his vast house with all his wives and children and con-
cubines, it seems probable that he had been up to the
same sort of tricks as Colebrooke.

The Government at Calcutta acted on Trevelyan's
proposals with great speed. They stopped the prosecution of his agent, suspended Colebrooke and appointed
two commissioners to investigate the charges against
him. Sir Charles Metcalfe probably had a hand in this,
as his brother had doubtless kept him posted with what
was happening. The Government were also probably
influenced by the fact that Colebrooke had been suspended some years before on similar charges. Bentinck,
the Governor-General, was a liberal reformer, and was
presumably temperamentally inclined to favour Trevelyan's side of the case against the prevailing local British
opinion.

The Colebrookes continued their efforts to blacken
Trevelyan's name. Lady Colebrooke circulated a round
robin to the officers of three regiments and the civil
officials in Delhi:

Lady Colebrooke begs to take this mode of appeal-
ing to the public and of leaving them to form their

opinion of the base and dishonourable conduct of
Mr Trevelyan, who is found to have been plot-
ting and fabricating falsehoods against her, and
clandestinely transmitting them to the Government
for several months past, during which he was par-
taking of Sir Edward's hospitality. Lady Colebrooke
cannot but think that *liar* and *villain* are the mildest
terms which can be applied to such an act of
depravity in so young a man.

The Government of India had appointed Fraser,
the next senior officer, to act in Colebrooke's place
and Fraser did his best to help Colebrooke by ordering
that everything should go on much as before, that the
business should be carried on in Colebrooke's name
and that there should be no public sign that Colebrooke
had been suspended. 'The reality is sufficiently painful
to me,' he wrote, 'and needs not display to make it
more so.' Trevelyan cannot be blamed for resorting
to deception at this point. He told Fraser that he would
obey the orders with scrupulous attention and would
avoid any demonstration of authority that might upset
Colebrooke; but at the same time he reported the situation to Calcutta, with the result that Fraser too was
suspended. Colebrooke now felt the net closing in on
him. He went on abusing Trevelyan as a spy and
informer, ending one of his tirades with, 'Let me only
retire where the sound of his name may never insult
my ears. I may say, with the frogs pelted by the boys,
what is sport to you is death to me.'
    The commissioners arrived from Calcutta and began
their inquiry. Colebrooke wrote a long memorandum
in which he attacked Trevelyan and his supporters
and tried to suggest that he himself had only been
doing what Sir Charles Metcalfe had done before him.
Trevelyan replied with a detailed refutation of Colebrooke's attack. They threw Latin tags and abusive
similes at each other. Colebrooke described Thomas

Metcalfe as 'the ass who approached to add his kick at
the sick lion'. Trevelyan replied:

> Sir E. Colebrooke, I perceive, compares himself to
> the lion. I am at a loss to conjecture in what respect
> thcy resemble each other, except in their voracity.
> The sickness he alludes to proceeds, I presume, from
> surfeit; a disgorgement would probably relieve it.
> The comparison that most obviously presents itself,
> is that of a fox who, chased from his sanctuary, baffled
> in all his wiles, run down and hopeless of escape,
> employs what strength he has left in endeavouring
> to inflict wounds of some sort or other upon his
> adversaries.

Colebrooke's dishonesty was clear. The commissioners found against him; he was dismissed from the
Residency and subsequently from the service. The
directors wrote that they accepted with regret Bentinck's recommendation that Colebrooke should not be
prosecuted. Prominent Indians had been involved and
the Government did not want to put them into the
witness-box. Trevelyan prepared a complete statement
of the affair, which he wanted to publish, but Bentinck
advised him not to, since Colebrooke had been fully
exposed and could do no more harm. He had therefore to content himself with printing it and sending it
round to his friends. He was already showing that propensity to publish his views which was to get him into
trouble on several occasions during his career.

Officially the affair had ended in Trevelyan's complete triumph. He received the highest praise from
the Governor-General and from the directors. All he
asked as a reward was an appointment for his brother,
and that was two years later. In the letter informing
him that his request had been granted, Bentinck wrote
that Trevelyan had a strong claim on him as Governor-
General and referred to his manly conduct in standing

forth, single and alone, to rescue the character of his Service and his country from disgrace. Even allowing for the high-flown style of the period, the terms of Bentinck's praise were such as can surely never have been addressed to any other Indian Civilian in his mid-twenties by a Governor-General. Trevelyan was now marked out as an outstanding member of the Civil Service.

But he had passed through a bad time. Only a very tough and resilient character could have come through it undaunted. Macaulay afterwards wrote: 'A perfect storm was raised against the accuser. He was almost everywhere abused and generally cut. But with a firmness and ability scarcely ever seen in one so young, he brought his proofs forward and fully made out his case.' He had written to his mother soon after the outcome of the struggle was clear:

I have of course exasperated all Sir Edward Cole-brooke's personal friends and the whole of the old school of Indian corruption. You must therefore expect, my dear mother, to hear no ordinary abuse of me from these two classes, particularly as the Cole-brookes are intimately connected with your family and as most of your 'Indian' friends belong to a period when the acts for which Sir Edward Colebrooke has been brought to trial were looked upon in a very indulgent light, and they cannot therefore but consider my interference as presumptuous and uncalled for.

But he added that he had some good friends who had stuck by him.

Imagination and enterprise were among Trevelyan's qualities. Before he left Delhi he bought with his own money an area of waste land outside the Lahore Gate and laid it out in streets and squares, giving to applicants as much land as they required to build houses. The scheme was successful and the suburb was known as Trevelyanganj. It is now lost in a maze of the streets of Old Delhi, though it is identified in maps of Delhi's history.

It was clearly time for him to move on from Delhi and he was appointed political agent at Kotah in Rajputana, with responsibility also for the neighbouring State of Bundi. He wrote a lively account for his mother of a foray in Bundi arising out of the murder of the State minister. The murderers, with a hundred and fifty of their supporters, had taken refuge in a house in Bundi town. The Raja of Bundi fired his guns at the house and the Jodhpuris, who were on the side of the besieged men, started to collect their forces to attack Bundi, which would have meant much killing and looting. Trevelyan was some miles away in Kotah. Hearing guns firing, he galloped off by himself and arrived in Bundi just in time to stop the Jodhpuris' attack, threatening them that if they advanced towards Bundi, he would have them 'cut up to a man'. He got the men out of the house by giving all except the actual murderers a safe conduct, and the Jodhpuris dispersed, while the Raja of Bundi was satisfied by being able to execute the murderers. Trevelyan had a right to be pleased with himself and had obviously thoroughly enjoyed the affair.

He was beginning to form ideas on political policy. He advocated a generous policy towards the princes and described the current policy towards them as 'very cold, unamiable and unproductive of beneficial results'. Not surprisingly, he was a little arrogant, at least in writing to his brother, declaring that he would not float through life, but would conquer. He realised that he would not live down his unpopularity among the British community over the Colebrooke affair, or advance in the service by staying in the obscurity of Rajputana. So in 1831 he applied for and was given the post of deputy secretary in the Political Department at Calcutta. He was now a formidable young man, favoured in high places, with the Colebrooke affair behind him, not desk-bound, but an enterprising and courageous young political officer and reputedly one of the best pig-stickers in India. But his interests were predominantly in public affairs. He was already taking an interest in freeing internal trade and had written a preliminary report on the subject which was to absorb much of his time during the next few years, the right path for Indian education, which was to have a major influence on the development of Indian political life.

4

CALCUTTA AND THE MACAULAYS

CHARLES TREVELYAN remained in Calcutta for seven years, during which time the course of his life was changed by his marriage to Hannah More Macaulay, who had accompanied her brother to his Indian appointment as member of the Supreme Council. When they had reached Madras, Macaulay had stopped for a tour in the south, sending Hannah on to Calcutta. He joined her there at the beginning of October and in mid-November they were established in the house which later became well known to many generations of Englishmen as the Bengal Club. Before Christmas Hannah and Charles Trevelyan were married.

Macaulay was devoted, almost to excess, to his two sisters, Margaret Cropper and Hannah. He wrote to Margaret about the engagement, but she had died before the letter reached England. In that letter he had written that Hannah was marrying with his warmest approbation, and that if he had had to search India for a husband for her he could have found no man to whom he could with equal confidence have entrusted her happiness. Trevelyan had distinguished himself beyond any man of his standing by his great talent for business, his liberal and enlarged views of policy and by literary merit. He had been applauded in the highest terms by the Government of India and by the directors for his action against Colebrooke, and he was considered likely to rise to the very top of the service.

Macaulay gave a vivid picture of the young bridegroom :

Trevelyan is a most stirring reformer. His reading has been very confined; but to the little that he has read, he has brought a mind as active and restless as Lord Brougham's, and much more judicious and honest. His principles I believe to be excellent and his temper very sweet. His own religious feelings are ardent, like all his feelings, even to enthusiasm, but he is by no means intolerant with regard to others. He is rash and uncompromising in public matters. If he were a wrong-headed and narrow-minded man, he would be a perfect nuisance. But he has so strong an understanding that, though he often goes too fast, he scarcely ever goes in a wrong direction. Lord William said to me : 'That man is almost always on the right side in every question, and it is well that he is so, for he gives most confounded trouble when he happens to take the wrong one.'

His manners are odd, blunt almost to roughness at times, and at other times awkward even to sheepishness. But when you consider that during the important years of his life, from twenty to twenty-five, he was in a remote province of India, where his whole time was divided between public business and field sports, and where he seldom saw a European gentleman and never a European lady, you will not wonder at this. There is nothing vulgar about him. He has no great tact or knowledge of the world, but these drawbacks, were they six times more serious, would be trifling compared with the excellencies of his character. Nobody can think him handsome. He has, however, a very good figure and always looks like a gentleman everywhere, but particularly on horseback. He is very active and athletic and is renowned as a great master in the most exciting and perilous of field sports, the spearing of wild boars. His face has a most characteristic expression of ardour and impetuosity. His mind is full of schemes of moral and political improvement and his zeal boils over in all his talk. His topics even in courtship are steam navigation, the education of the natives, the equalisation of the sugar duties, the substitution of the Roman for the Arabic alphabet in the oriental languages. He is by no means so good a wooer as a financier and diplomatist. He has had no practice, and he never read, I believe, a novel in all his life; so that his love-making, though very ardent and sincere, is as awkward as you could wish to see. He will not however be the worse husband on that account.

However much he approved of Trevelyan as a brother-in law, Macaulay was for a time shattered by the marriage of the second beloved sister and expressed himself in another letter to Margaret in what appears to us now as extravagant language:

Everything is dark. The world is a desert before me. I have nothing to love, nothing to live for. I have been prodigal of my love, and I have had the fate of other prodigals. My tenderness would have been more highly prized if it had been less lavishly given. This bitter lesson, which comes too late to be of any use, is all that I have got in exchange for the blighted hopes and squandered affections of a life.

Hannah and Charles realised something of what he was feeling. It was arranged that they would live with him so long as they were together in Calcutta. But it cannot have been an easy situation for the young bridegroom.

After the wedding, at which Lord and Lady William

Bentinck were present, probably very like our wedding in Delhi a hundred and three years later, the couple went off for a honeymoon at a cottage lent them by the Bentincks, but had to return early on the news of the death in England of Hannah's sister. This was another shattering blow for Macaulay and must have cast a gloom over the first months of Charles's married life. A few days after the wedding, Hannah wrote to Charles's mother: 'I must tell you what Lord William said of him to my brother; "His wife will give him the only thing he wants to make his character perfect, discretion."' But in that she did not succeed.

In his early years in Calcutta, Trevelyan had written a report of considerable importance on the abolition of the internal customs duties. Macaulay described it as a perfect masterpiece of its kind, the ablest state paper which he had read in India or England. But during those years Trevelyan's energies had been largely devoted to the cause of English education in India, a policy which, through the powerful advocacy of Macaulay, was adopted by the Government and changed the face of India. There is no doubt about the important part that this extraordinary young man played in the movement leading to this decision. The orientalists had had it all their own way until Trevelyan was appointed secretary of the General Committee of Public Instruction in 1833, the year before Macaulay arrived in Calcutta. The controversy then flared up and the committee reached a deadlock. Macaulay described Trevelyan as being at the head of that active party among the younger servants of the Company who took the side of improvement, and as the soul of every scheme for diffusing education among Indians. He wrote that when he arrived in Calcutta, he found Trevelyan engaged in a furious contest against half a dozen of the oldest and most powerful men in India on the subject. 'I thought him a little rash in his expressions, but in essentials quite right. I joined him, threw

all my influence into his scale, brought over Lord
William to declare himself, and thus I have, I hope,
been the means of effecting some real good.'

The question was, in Macaulay's words, 'whether the
funds employed by Government for the purposes of
education should be employed in teaching Arabic and
Sanskrit, the medicine of Galen, the astronomy of
Ptolemy and the fables of the Hindu mythologists, or
in communicating European knowledge by means of
the English language. There was not a single question
which did not resolve itself into the one great question :
English or Sanskrit, Newton or Ptolemy, the Vedas or
Adam Smith, the Mahabharata or Milton, the sun
round the earth or the earth round the sun, the medicine of the Middle Ages or the medicine of the nineteenth century.' The Government's decision was based
on Macaulay's famous minute of January 1835, but
Trevelyan had been preparing the way for some years.
In 1834 he had published the pamphlet which he had
written in his leisure hours in Kotah. He was already
thinking in broad political terms and without political
illusions. In one of his many writings on the subject
he argued that the British had nothing to give the
Indians except their superior knowledge. Everything
else – revenues, honours, private emoluments – was
taken from them, but in the end the greater proportion of the advantages which the British gained would
be amply repaid.

In 1838 Trevelyan published an essay giving his
mature thoughts on the subject. In it he faced the long-
term consequences of the decision. He refuted the argument that the British should not educate the Indians,
since by giving them knowledge they would be given
power, of which they would make the first use against
the British. If British interest and duty were really
opposed to each other, every honest Englishman would
know which to prefer. Our national experience had
given us too deep a sense of the true ends of Govern-

ment to allow us to think of carrying on the administration of India except for the benefit of the people of India. A nation which had made a great sacrifice by abolishing slavery could never think of keeping Indians in ignorance by means of a political system supported by revenues taken from the Indians themselves. We should look not to the duration of our trust, but to the satisfactory discharge of it.

But in this case our interest and duty were the same. The connection between India and England could not in the nature of things be permanent; Indians would ultimately regain their independence. There were two ways of arriving at this point: through revolution or through reform. A sudden and violent revolution would end in a complete alienation of mind and separation of interests; gradual and peaceful reform would end in a permanent alliance founded on mutual benefit and goodwill. If this course were adopted, a precarious and temporary relation would pass into another far more durable and beneficial. Trained by us to happiness and independence, India would remain the proudest monument of British benevolence and we would continue to reap, in the affectionate attachment of the people and in a great commercial intercourse, the fruit of that liberal and enlightened policy which suggested to us this line of conduct. He drew a historical parallel in the policy of Julius Agricola to instruct the sons of the leading men among the Britons in the literature and science of Rome. From being obstinate enemies, the Britons soon became attached to the Romans, and made more strenuous efforts to retain them than their own ancestors had to resist the Roman invasion. It would be a shame to us if we also did not make our premature departure dreaded as a calamity. 'It must not be said in after ages that the groans of the Britons were elicited by the breaking up of the Roman Empire and the groans of the Indians by the continued existence of the British.'

This was a splendid declaration of policy, and was also sound political sense. The revolution looking back to the old Indian kingdoms came, but was not successful, since it had only partial support. Later political complications – the changes in the pattern of world power, the terrible wars of the twentieth century – could not be foreseen, but, by and large, the essential pattern of the transfer of political power emerged as Trevelyan had foreshadowed it and there is no doubt that the education policy of 1835, which gave educated Indians access to English liberal political thought, was largely responsible for the way in which the Indian independence movement developed. This event, almost forgotten today, truly changed the destiny of India.

It changed more. Trevelyan wrote that the English language would in time be spoken by millions in all the four quarters of the globe, and our learning and principles of constitutional liberty, diffused through the local languages, would spread far and wide among the nations. The example of the great countries colonised by British settlers may have been the main impulse towards the acceptance of English as the most widespread world language, but its adoption by India was a powerful ally and we can trace back to Lord William Bentinck's decision, so hotly contested in his council, the emergence of English as the common language of Asia, with all that that has brought in its train. With the departure of the British, Indians must modify their political system inherited from the British, but it is due to that inheritance, made possible by the diffusion of the English language, that India is still basically a democracy in tune with our ideas. It was a decision with profound consequences for the twentieth-century world.

In the later years of the independence movement, the Congress party used to stigmatise Macaulay's minute as an infamous attempt to bind the imperial system more firmly on India, and Mrs Gandhi recently said that though India benefited from the decision, those who were concerned in it did not realise that it would help towards Indian independence. This assumption is wholly untrue, as is seen from Charles Trevelyan's line of argument in his pamphlet. The policy has also been attacked as an attempt to supplant the Indian languages by English. That this was not the intention of the reformers is made clear in Trevelyan's essay. He wrote that the instruction of the mass of the people through their own language was the ultimate object to be kept in view. If this aim was lost sight of and the Indian languages were neglected, it was the fault of subsequent generations, British and Indians, who developed the system introduced in 1835. The reformers of that year were faced with a limited practical problem. The contest was between English on the one hand, and Arabic and Sanskrit on the other. The money to be spent on either was limited and there was not enough for both. In this framework there is surely little doubt that the decision was correct. If it had gone the other way, the British would have been accused with justification of having denied the Indians access to learning which would help them to form a modern state, and Nehru's view that the British had stood in the way of Indian education would have been justified.

Only in their expectation of concurrent social reform and the decline of Hinduism were the reformers wide of the mark. They underestimated the strength of Indian religion and customs and could not foresee the decline of Christianity in the West. Starting from the standpoint of dogmatic Christianity, they failed to see any good in the Hindu religion. Macaulay wrote to his father that he believed that if the plans for the development of education were followed up, there would not be a single idolator among the respectable classes in Bengal in thirty years' time, and that this would be effected without the smallest interference with religious liberty, merely by the natural operation of knowledge and reflection. Trevelyan wrote that Hinduism was so entirely destitute of evidence and was identified with so many gross immoralities and physical absurdities that it must give way at once before the light of European science. As the change wrought by the new education advanced, India would become quite another country. Nothing more would be heard of excitable religious feelings and priestcraft would no longer be able to work by ignorance. How wrong they were. We can understand how the reformers were blinded by their faith in the superiority of their own religion and way of life, and how they failed to understand the qualities of Hindu thought and the deep roots of Hinduism in the life of most Indians. We can see that the 'Orientals' in this controversy had much argument on their side. Yet, on balance, they were surely wrong and the 'Europeans' right.

The Trevelyans were to remain very close to Macaulay until his death twenty-five years later. Macaulay found it a very monotonous life. He wrote to another sister that breakfasts, councils, airings, dinners, sleep, waking, followed each other in a rotation which was only now and then slightly interrupted by a great formal banquet which some great man gave to thirty or forty people. By the end of 1835 a girl had been born and Macaulay was beginning to recover from the shock of Margaret's death. He soon began to take an interest in the child's development, apparently expecting genius to blossom in a few months and seeking excuses for the baby being unable to speak when ten months old; in particular that she heard familiar objects described in two languages. So the family life went on smoothly until January 1838 when they all went home together, Macaulay having acquired the 'modest competence' which he considered necessary for his English career and the Trevelyans on furlough, intending an early return to India.

In 1836 Trevelyan had accepted an unrewarding appointment as secretary to the Board of Revenue. This earned him the approbation of Lord Auckland, who had followed Bentinck as Governor-General, and who commended Trevelyan for thinking of the public service and not of himself. Trevelyan was absorbed in public business, but found time to develop his habit of writing for the press on current affairs, using the pseudonym 'Indophilus' which he was to adopt again in England. We learn from the letter of a family friend that his arguments were levelled at the oppressive nature of the taxation which had been adopted by the British Government in India, and which had the effect of paralysing the industry and energies of the people. It was a foretaste of an Indian controversy to come. Macaulay summed up Trevelyan's character by quoting Julius Caesar on Brutus: 'Magni refert hic quid velit; sed quidquid volet, valde volet.' Indeed, he became passionately involved in the issues which he took up, but, as Bentinck had said, was generally on the right side.

Trevelyan had made a great reputation in India. Before he left, Colvin, a fellow civilian who was to die in Agra during the Mutiny, wrote to tell him how glad he was to hear from Macaulay that Trevelyan intended to return to India, since they could ill afford to spare a gifted and energetic spirit by whom so much had been accomplished. 'You have effected in the course of half your career what far exceeds the performance of the longest service of many of our ablest and most honoured public servants.' Trevelyan's Indian life had been marked by his own courage and initiative, but he could have been ruined without the consistent support of one of the greatest English figures on the Indian stage, Lord William Bentinck. Trevelyan afterwards said that to him belonged the great praise of having placed our dominion in India on its proper foundation in the recognition of the great principle that India is to be governed for the benefit of Indians. Macaulay's famous tribute was engraved on Bentinck's statue in Calcutta. For once, an official tribute was true.

5

PUBLIC AFFAIRS AT HOME

CHARLES TREVELYAN did not return to India for twenty-one years. He was appointed assistant secretary to the Treasury, in effect the head of the department, presumably through the influence of Macaulay wanting to keep his beloved sister in England. So the Indian rumour which Colvin had heard, that he would not go back after his furlough, proved true. His semi-official correspondence during this period is recorded in eleven thousand pages in thirty-eight stout volumes of letter-books. He was an immensely hard worker and spared neither himself nor others. In a time of stress he sent his family away, shut up his house in Grosvenor Crescent, and went into lodgings near his office, starting work at 6 a.m. and sometimes even at 3 a.m. His achievement during these years was formidable and he has been given the credit for creating the basis of modern Treasury practice. He busied himself about everything that came to his notice. He built up the Treasury library and made sure that the civil servants used it. He criticised the style of his officials' minutes and advised them what authors to read to improve it. He was apt to give advice on matters not his concern and did not always respect other people's feelings. With all his energy and drive and his immense capacity for mastering the facts of a situation, his weakness was his passion for going into detail, not always relevant to the case.

His administration of the Irish famine has been strongly attacked. He was not responsible for the policy, but, as a civil servant, for its execution, though he undoubtedly influenced policy, which was based on the prevalent *laissez faire* view of economics. We may now think this to have been unsuited as a basis for relieving the terrible distress of those years, but the men of that period were neither callous nor careless and were convinced that they were doing their best for the Irish people. There was no doubt of the Government's view of his handling of the situation. He was commended in the most flattering terms and given a K.C.B. and a year's salary as a reward. From this point I call him Sir Charles. He was deeply distressed by public attacks on him at the time, and Peel wrote to reassure him that his resolute and honest discharge of duty would in the end receive the approbation of those whose judgement was worth having. He had himself no doubts that he had been right. In accordance with his usual practice he wrote a pamphlet on the Irish crisis, which he sent to, among others, the King of Prussia, the Pope and, many years later, the Viceroy, Lord Northbrook, to help him cope with the Indian famine of 1873.

During the first year of the Crimean war he was responsible for the commissariat, which was generally held to have failed to provide proper supplies for the army in the field. He does not seem to have been criticised himself, but took pains to vindicate the commissariat officers before the select committee examining its shortcomings. He was an exacting master, but loyal to his subordinates. His association with the army in the Crimea led to a long friendship with Florence Nightingale, who would end a letter exclusively devoted to the sanitary arrangements of the troops in India by subscribing herself, 'Yours gratefully and affectionately'.

In November 1853, in collaboration with Stafford
Northcote, he produced the report which, after a period
of controversy, created the civil service as we know
it today. His efforts to destroy the patronage system
did not prevent him from making frequent applica-
tions in England and India for posts for his and
Macaulay's relations, but it would be wrong to regard
this as qualifying Macaulay's description of him as a
man of rigid integrity, or as being inconsistent with his
views on patronage, since so long as the patronage
system remained, it was the normal way in which posts
were filled. With his principles, he would not have proposed anyone not fit for the job.

During all this period of controversy he was becoming a very experienced and tough fighter for his ideas,
abused by the opponents of reform, but earning personal respect. Trollope, in his autobiography, related
how he had introduced Sir Charles Trevelyan, as he
was by that time, into *The Three Clerks* in the
character of Sir Gregory Hardlines, for the purpose
of attacking 'that much loathed scheme of competitive
examination'. Later he came to know Charles and
Hannah, and wrote that though he never learned to
love competitive examination, he became very fond
of Trevelyan.

Sir Charles's habit of writing to the press, from
which he was to suffer the greatest setback in his career,
was already getting him into trouble. He made Peel
very angry by publishing two long letters predicting
a rebellion in Ireland fomented by Catholic priests,
and abusing O'Connell, immediately after making a
confidential report on the state of Ireland to Peel and
Sir James Graham and without consulting them. After
publication of the first letter, Graham protested to
him, but he was totally unmoved and promptly published the second. During the controversy over civil
service reform, he was using the press to further his
views and encouraging Northcote to do the same. Glad-

stone, obviously perturbed, wrote to him to ensure that he would not indulge his predilection for publicity without Gladstone's agreement.

I am only concerned with Sir Charles Trevelyan's Indian career and opinions, but I have touched briefly on these twenty-one years of his official life at home, since during this period of restless activity the forceful, controversial character of his second Indian period was being formed. He was now the most prominent Whitehall official; still, in Bentinck's words twenty years before, almost always on the right side in every question, but giving most confounded trouble when he happened to take the wrong one. He was well known to the great mid-Victorian political figures, Peel, Palmerston, Disraeli, Gladstone, Northcote, and especially to Sir Charles Wood, afterwards the first Viscount Halifax, who was Chancellor of the Exchequer and thus Charles's direct superior during the anxious days of the Irish famine, and later President of the Board of Control. Wood became a close personal friend and was to be intimately concerned with the peaks and troughs of Trevelyan's later Indian life.

Throughout this period Sir Charles retained an active interest in Indian affairs. He advised Wood over the last renewal of the Company's charter, his comprehensive scheme of educational reform and his plans for the development of railways and irrigation which were subsequently interrupted by the Mutiny. The Charter Act of 1853 stripped the Company of its commercial character, but extended its administrative powers. It was widely debated whether the Company should be abolished and the Government take over full responsibility for the administration of India. This was Disraeli's view, but both Wood and Sir Charles were opposed to it, basing their objections on the theory of what they called 'double Government', in this case a check by the Company on the actions of Parliament. Sir Charles urged the unfitness of the people as represented in Parliament to wield unchecked power over India. He held that India had to be protected from the selfishness and rapacity of human nature which found free scope under the elastic machinery of a representative government. He was a Whig, but no radical. The high Tories did not want a change. Derby wanted to keep his party together, and so the Company's existence was continued for another eight years, until it was finally extinguished by the Mutiny.

He took a prominent part in the introduction of competitive examinations for the Indian civil service, parallel with his work with Northcote on the civil service at home. At first, competition was introduced only for entry through Haileybury, the old East India Company's college where he had been trained; but the academics, Jowett of Balliol and Vaughan of Harrow, intervened in order to get a share of the appointments for the universities and, with the help of Sir Charles, who enlisted Macaulay's influence and persuasive pen, convinced Wood that Haileybury should not be the exclusive channel for Indian appointments and, in the end, that it should cease to be an Indian College. Thus the 'competition wallahs' were born.

The House of Lords' committee on Indian affairs in 1853 gave Sir Charles the opportunity as an expert witness to express his mature views on a variety of Indian questions. The most striking part of his evidence was his reading of a paper written for him by a retired Indian civilian, who wrote that in his early service the country had been unsettled and disturbed, and the British had had to depend on Indians of power and influence to keep things tolerably quiet. They were therefore obliged to be civil and kind to the people. Since that time the British had become much stronger and no one dreamed of opposing them. They treated Indians worse and had ceased to live at all familiarly with them.

Most civil servants and military officers had embraced

extreme religious opinions and looked down on Indians as pagans, in addition to their racial prejudices. He had known a civil officer make the Indian officials and his own servants attend family worship in English, which was absurd, and a commanding officer stop the Hindus honouring the colours with garlands and incense, a custom as old as the Indian army. That regiment had subsequently mutinied. The fountains in the Government gardens at Agra were turned off on Sundays, although it was a favourite resort of the Indian community on that day. The Government had shown a dangerous partiality for the missionaries and had been known to intervene improperly in their favour in court cases. Among the Mohammedans pledges had been exchanged to rise if forcible conversion were attempted. The fear was illusory, but its existence was an element of danger. Attempts to force prisoners of different castes to mess together had caused outbreaks and loss of life in the gaols. If by the imprudence of Government a spirit of religious patriotism were once excited in India, and if it got into the army, British power would be at an end. The only safe and just policy was perfect neutrality in religion. His warnings were proved well-founded four years later in 1857.

Retired Indian civil servants of all generations would have ruefully confirmed Sir Charles's analysis of their situation. He said that many 'civilians' had worked in complete obscurity for many years in order to satisfy their consciences and do their duty by the Indians. He described how, when a civil servant who had performed the most important functions in India, returned home, he was less known than people of no importance or merit whatsoever in England, so that he was subjected to the threefold trial of descending from a state of power to a state of absence of influence, from a state of mental activity to a state of inaction, and from a position of importance to insecurity and insignificance. He had often heard his colleagues say, 'Whatever

sacrifices we make, however many years we may suffer
the inconveniences and risks of a bad climate, whatever good service we may do, when we go home we are
nobody, we are utterly unknown.' His plea was for
more honours, which he described as a cheap and effective way of stimulating and rewarding merit. The army
got enough, particularly from the Sikh and Afghan
campaigns, but civilians were never given honours for
work in the ordinary administration or judicial service.

In reply to questions on the effect of educating
Indians on British power, he developed the ideas which
he had propounded in India in the thirties. The alternative was between education leading to independence
after an indefinite period in circumstances happy for
both England and India, and government of India for
the benefit only of the British employed there, leading
to earlier independence in much less happy circumstances. The best way of keeping the Indian empire
was to educate Indians to hold responsible posts in an
administration which everyone would admire. It was
good common sense and neatly cut the ground from
under their Lordships' feet.

Like the civil servant whose views he had quoted, he
firmly supported the view that the Government of
India should observe complete religious neutrality.
Christianity would prevail, but it would suffer if it
were officially patronised by a conquering Government.
The missionaries would get on better on their own.
This also was good common sense, but he was still
underrating the strength of the Indian religions. There
was a comic touch in the Bishop of Oxford's concern
lest the instruction of the Hindus in oriental literature
should make them acquainted with 'the most impure
writings which exist in the world'. Sir Charles replied
that he had read the *Bhagavadgita* several times with
pleasure and had not found anything impure in it.

He showed himself to be a man of sympathy and
understanding in deploring the tendency to speak dis-

paragingly about Anglo-Indians. They had, he said, a claim on us, being our descendants. They were in an equivocal position, were not owned by either community and were therefore sensitive, but they had much of the good qualities of both races. There was another comic touch in Lord Ellenborough's suggestion that 'the ladies of this class were physically much better than the men', to which he replied primly that that was not borne out by his observation.

He developed two favourite themes of his later Indian period in his attack on the state of law between the European settlers and Indians, which gave the settlers an unfair and improper advantage; and in his passionate advocacy of a free press, to which civil servants, who were unpractised speakers but very apt with their pens, should be allowed to contribute, drawing on his experience of the results of his own letters to the press in India.

His evidence gives a revealing account of the issues affecting relations between British and Indians in the mid-century. He had begun by recounting that the qualities which Indians admired in the British were not our civilisation and material achievements; but they would say: 'Yes, you are a wonderful people; you speak the truth; you keep to your word. When you have promised a thing, however injurious it may be to you, you observe it; you hold by it generation after generation.' He ended by praising the country, people and civilisation of India and looked forward to an India, educated in English, informed by free discussion and adopting Christianity of its own free will, working changes far and wide through the countries and islands of Asia. Much of his interest was still directed to India.

6

ECHOES OF THE MUTINY

T H E Mutiny was naturally most disturbing for any man living in England with experience of Indian service. Sir Charles Trevelyan, always eager to express his feelings in print, published a long series of letters on Indian affairs in *The Times*, using his old pseudonym of Indophilus. He declared that God had honoured our nation above every other by entrusting to it the destiny of India, and we had been criminally indifferent to the trust. He was greatly distressed at the news of the death of his old friend, John Colvin, during the attack on Agra, describing him as one of the last of our Indian statesmen who derived their inspiration by immediate tradition from Malcolm, Munro, Metcalfe and Bentinck.

He continued that those master-builders had completed the edifice of our Indian empire on the solid foundations of good faith, justice and personal respect. Many of their disciples had devoted themselves to the interests of the Indians with self-denying zeal. Painful symptoms had, however, appeared of over-confidence arising from habitual success, of the pride which goes before a fall, and especially of a disposition to undervalue Indians and to be indifferent to their feelings, which alone would disqualify us from the government of India. Incredible though it seemed, the practice had grown up of calling Indians 'niggers', and it was evident from the surprise expressed by Indians who found themselves being decently treated on a visit to England, that they were being very differently treated by Englishmen in the East. It was strange that the Government of India had allowed these practices to grow up. If we did not change our ways, there would be another and much worse mutiny and that would be the end of our empire in India.

There was, however, in his eyes one favourable result of the Mutiny. The discipline of the Bengal army had been dangerously relaxed and the necessary reforms had been blocked by strong professional prejudice. But an unexpected stroke had come from the hand of the Almighty. The Bengal army had ceased to exist. We had therefore a golden opportunity to reconstitute the army on a safe, efficient and economical footing, with the final result of converting an annual deficit into an annual surplus and of developing Indian resources by a state of assured peace, improved administration and well executed public works. He had followed this line of argument in a letter in which he had written that, although Ireland had been connected with us for centuries, her social state had been a mystery to us until it was laid bare by a wonderful stroke of Providence, which could surely only have referred to the Irish famine. Truly, in his mind, God worked in a mysterious way his wonders to perform.

He was no sentimentalist. He related how the thugs had decided not to strangle Europeans because the Europeans carried arms, but very seldom money, and because if they strangled a single European, they would never hear the last of it. The latter reason was the real motive, and what we had to do was to impress the same opinion indelibly on the whole of India, since there was no other way for a handful of foreigners to keep their rule over millions of Indians. Mutineers captured in arms must be punished, but he warned that if the punishment exceeded the necessity of the case, a rebound would take place to the detriment of the judge.

He discussed what should be done with Delhi. Many were crying, 'Delenda est Carthago,' but he advocated God's reply to Jonah: 'Should not I spare Nineveh, that great city, wherein are more than six score thousand persons that cannot discern between their right hand and their left hand, and also much cattle?' However, he had no feeling for the beauty of the Red Fort and recommended that the palace, 'that sink of iniquity and rallying point of every hostile influence', should be razed to the ground, and a strong citadel erected on its ruins. This would contain our magazines, artillery, treasury and the barracks of the European troops, and it might be called Fort Victoria, as an emblem of the final establishment of our power in the interior of India. Fortunately his idea was not adopted, though barracks were built on part of the site, which overlook and dwarf those exquisite pavilions and gardens subsequently restored by Lord Curzon.

During the later months of the Mutiny, his friends in the thick of it in India found time to write to him their views of the tragic events of those years. John Lawrence wrote that they had been passing through a frightful ordeal and it was by God's mercy alone that any Englishman was alive on that side of India. The British had been as much to blame as the people. He was convinced that there had been no conspiracy outside the army, and even in it, one could scarcely say there was a conspiracy. The army had been in an unsatisfactory state for a long time, but the immediate cause was undoubtedly the cartridge question.* It was an affair of caste, of personal impurity. Both Hindus and Mohammedans believed that we meant by a bit of legerdemain to make them all Christians.

---

* The sepoys believed that their cartridges were greased with pig fat and therefore polluted them. In fact, they were not made to use the greased cartridges anywhere except in one place in Sind.

Lawrence developed his ideas on Christianity in India. He thought that it would be possible to introduce the bible into schools without any trouble, since, with the exception of a few Maulvis and Pundits, the people had no longer any regard for their religion and would not care, so long as we did not interfere with their caste prejudices and ritual observances. No great change could be effected among them except by a change of religion. There would have been no mutiny if the people had understood more of our religion and if the English had set them a better example in obeying its precepts. It was those who had least understood our views who had been our enemies. The people as a mass had not been against us.

It is strange to us, over a hundred years later, to read of Lawrence's confidence in the conversion of India to Christianity as a practical policy, however much we may agree with his diagnosis that the Mutiny was largely caused by the stupidity of the foreign Christians, coupled with the appalling condition of the Bengal army in which, as he wrote, reform was impracticable, since the officers would not admit that any was necessary and nobody not in the army was supposed to know anything about it.

Both Lawrence and Sir Richard Temple told Sir Charles that the stories of atrocities had been exaggerated. Lawrence thought it probable that some Englishwomen had been raped, but wrote that at Delhi they were cut down as soon as found, and the stories that young girls had been crucified, hanging by the hair and the like, were not true. Temple reported that people who would have known, had not heard of any case of mutilation, that a man whom he had read of in England as dying a horrible death, was alive and uninjured, and that the 32nd regiment believed that their women had not been maltreated. He gave details of several horror stories which had been proved to be untrue and thought that not more than four or five women had been raped at Delhi. 'The rebels at most places were thirsty for blood and murdered quick.'

Lawrence was concerned about the reports of retaliation by the British. Murderers and the leaders of the Mutiny should be punished, but he saw every danger of justice degenerating into savage revenge. Already he had heard of strange deeds perpetrated by private individuals at Delhi and elsewhere, and it looked too like a general war of white man against black. There was little fear that offenders would escape the just penalty of their crimes; there was much that innocent people would suffer.

Lawrence was also very critical of military policy and tactics. Sir Colin Campbell was a fine, stout old soldier, who would prove too much for all open enemies, but he had neither the capacity nor the inclination to do all that had to be done. They had inadequate troops for the subjection of the country, if they were to wage a war of extermination. But strong measures appeared to be the order of the day. Everybody called out for war to the knife, never seeming to see that they had not the means of carrying out such a policy. No mutineer would surrender, for directly he was caught, he was hanged. Naturally enough, they all desired to die fighting. He was inclined to think that if hopes were held out of personal security to the least guilty of the mutineers, they would come in, give up their arms and go to their homes. They could then be kept under police surveillance and in the meantime, there would be breathing space to hunt the desperadoes, the murderers of our women and children. So long as all were classed together, they would all hold together and resist to the death.

Both Lawrence and Temple were preaching the need for reform and reorganisation. Temple wrote in February 1859, when it was all over, that many thought that the Indian Government had not the ways and means of carrying on affairs. Lawrence, he wrote, began to 'despair of the republic'. He did not, but he saw many defects, financial extravagance, the failure to select fit men for command, the incautious raising of Indian levies. He feared that the temper of the people had been thoroughly demoralised. To keep them in order, a European force would be required larger than the country could afford. Far too large a proportion of Indian troops would still be retained. Administrative and financial reform would not be introduced. Hindustan continued to be in a sad state. With this in his mind, Sir Charles Trevelyan set out again for India.

7

THE GOVERNMENT OF
MADRAS

IN January 1859 Sir Charles Trevelyan was offered
and accepted the post of Governor of Madras by Lord
Stanley, who described it as offering one of the widest
fields of usefulness that man could desire and as requiring a more active and energetic spirit. Sir Charles Wood,
who was to take over the India Office in a few months
when the Government changed, recorded his approval
of the appointment. Macaulay did not approve. The
family was going to be split, though Hannah for the
time being was going to stay at home with the children.
He described it as a most unhappy event. Their friends
were showing an utter want of sympathy by pestering
them with congratulations. The family was miserable.
Trevelyan, he wrote, was under a delusion. All his
virtues and his faults were brought strongly out, and,
between ambition and public spirit, he was as much
excited and as unfit to be reasoned with as if he had
drunk three bottles of champagne. But his elation, like
the elation produced by champagne, would soon be
over. A reaction would come and he would have very
much to suffer.

Sir Charles wrote to Canning, the Governor-General,
that he hoped Canning would find him a helpful and

obedient Governor. If Canning knew anything of Sir Charles's ways, he must have had his doubts about the obedience. Stanley made a suggestion which was bound to cause trouble. He asked Sir Charles to look into the question whether the supervision by the central over the provincial governments was not too minute, causing a waste of time rather than really saving money. Sir Charles was not the man to overlook that opportunity.

From his letters to Hannah we have a glimpse of him on the voyage. He wrote that he had committed himself to God, believing that he had been prepared and called for what was before him. His sense of mission was strong. He missed Hannah's literary guidance, feeling without her 'sadly at a loss to make out a fact or quotation'. He had forgotten the dates of the children's birthdays, including the dates of little Harriet's birth and death in Calcutta. He told Hannah that there was a good set of clergymen and ladies on board. Not all the ladies were first-rate, but the best gave tone to the others. He was highly circumspect in his dealings with them. 'Miss Falconer turned out to be a well-brought-up girl to whom I was able to pay such attention as our relative position required without fear of committing myself to anything questionable or disagreeable. Engaged ladies going to join their husbands are both safe and pleasant company.' In one department of life, at least, he did not take risks.

On his arrival at Madras he disclaimed in elaborately complimentary language the credit due to his predecessor for his labours, and especially for his judicious selection of men to be at the head of new departments. He must have changed his mind very quickly, for soon after, his son wrote expressing his surprise that Sir Charles's predecessor should have appointed a bevy of incapables, and commending his father for having come down on them like a hawk on a flock of pigeons. Sir Charles dismissed the accountant general for mak-

ing money out of confidential information, exposed a
man who had been living free on a Raja for two years
and wrote home somewhat disingenuously that, while
he never complained of his predecessor, it was a fact
that he had had to wash Lord Harris's dirty clothes.
He had high hopes that the Chief Justice, whom he
could not dismiss and who never did a day's work, had
finally ruined his health through debauchery and
would retire, but the man unfortunately got better and
decided to continue what Sir Charles called his
scandalous official career.

He quickly set about introducing administrative
reforms. He reorganised the public works and revenue
departments and completed his predecessor's reorganisation of the police. He abolished the bad old habit
of impressment of labour, apparently without great
opposition from the European community who had
benefited from it. He settled the in'ams – grants of
land for religious purposes – giving the holders a secure
tenure, and created a freehold tenure in building and
plantation land. He worked out a scheme for unifica-
tion of the Queen's and Company's Courts, which had
formerly existed in a spirit of mutual antagonism – a
long overdue reform. He reorganised the system of
collecting land revenue and water rate, built or planned
irrigation works and improved local amenities, including the creation of a people's park in Madras. He
reduced the Madras army by disbanding or reducing
the size of regiments and abolishing recruiting depots
and two arsenals, all with the cordial cooperation of
old Sir Patrick Grant, the Commander-in-Chief, whom
he soon had in his pocket.

He was completely absorbed in local affairs. A minor
but significant innovation was the invitation of Indians
and Anglo-Indians to Government House. He applied
for a picture of the Queen for Government House, asking Wood to reflect what it was to be governed by an
abstraction. This started the series of royal portraits

from which governors and ambassadors have benefited
or suffered ever since. He embarked on an extensive
tour of the south, describing his visit to Pondicherry
as a remarkable act of self-denial, since he could neither
dance nor speak French. After some days in the Nilgiris
he recommended that the previous proposal to rename
Jakatalla Wellington should be carried out and that
Ootacamund should be renamed Victoria. Many
generations of British soldiers have known the relief
of a spell in Wellington, but those of us who have an
affection for the Ooty downs are thankful that they
kept their old name. It was an astonishing record of
restless activity and achievement in only just over a
year, which was widely recognised in India and at home
and remained in public memory in Madras until my
time there.

In one matter he suffered defeat. Mysore State had
been under British administration for thirty years and
the Ruler had resolved not to adopt an heir. Sir Charles
feared that, since Canning had told the Rulers of Mewar
and Benares that they could adopt, the Mysore Raja
might change his mind. As Governor of Madras he took
a very different view from that which he had held
about the princes when he was a young political officer
in Rajputana. He considered that Mysore should
become part of the Madras presidency, being surrounded by it and being an integral part of it as much
as identity of language, institutions and interest could
make it. Meanwhile, he believed that if relations with
Mysore were transferred from the Central Government
to Madras, he could stop the Ruler from adopting
without any fuss being caused, and could supervise the
State administration which he thought was being
neglected by the Central Government. It was an arguable case on administrative grounds, though more
doubtful as a matter of general policy. Wood agreed in
principle and old Sir Mark Cubbon, who had administered Mysore more or less as his own personal kingdom

for more years than anyone could remember, was informed of the decision. He was a wily old man and was not going to be pushed out easily.

It was at this time that the news of Macaulay's death reached India. Sir Charles tried to get Sid Mark onto his own ground. He invited Sir Mark to stay at Government House, Madras, baiting the invitation with the statement that Macaulay, who had met Cubbon for a few days in 1834, had been highly impressed by him and often talked about him. Sir Mark had no intention of putting his head into the den of the man who wanted to swallow his beloved Mysore and throw him out into the bargain. He replied in absurdly extravagant language, as if he meant it to be seen that he was making a counter move, to the effect that he could not accept the invitation for the time being, since he was so deeply affected by Macaulay's death. He ended with an oblique statement about Indian duplicity, the meaning of which was probably that if Sir Charles thought he could handle the Mysoreans better than Sir Mark, he was very much mistaken. Twenty-five years before, Macaulay had commented on Sir Mark's extravagant language in praising Sir Charles's report on the transit dues. It was a technique perfected by long practice.

Cubbon then told Canning and sent in his resignation. Wood, with extraordinary carelessness, had ordered the transfer of a large State from the Central to a provincial government, without even telling the Governor-General. Canning was furious that his authority was being undermined and dug his toes in. So Wood had to give way. Cubbon had won. Two years later the administration of Mysore was transferred to the Ruler and in due course he adopted an heir. His descendants remain Maharajas of Mysore to this day. No one who has since had experience of the Mysore administration can regret the decision, though, after independence, Sir Charles's proposal was in effect carried out with the integration of all the Canaresespeaking districts as a unit of the Indian Federation.

During his first few months in Madras, Sir Charles was getting inflated ideas without a wife to bring him down to earth. He wrote to Hannah that power suited him, that the local newspapers did nothing but praise him and that he was getting on excellently with the Commander-in-Chief and the civil officials, because they could see that he knew what he was about. He soon came up against Canning, who had been distinctly cold from the start and had neither answered Sir Charles's letter from England nor sent him a letter of welcome to Madras. Canning's first letter was thoroughly unpleasant, rebuking Sir Charles for usurping the authority of the Central Government. Sir Charles apologised and Canning let the matter drop with rather bad grace. He would not have been pleased by Sir Charles's patronising remark in a letter to Stanley that Canning had acted with moderation and good sense.

Hannah soon heard stories in England that he was ignoring his official advisers and colleagues, and told him so. He was unabashed and pugnacious. It was the work of the 'Calcutta party'. He had gone down into the ring with them and given them a Cornish throw. Everybody must act according to his own genius. His principle through life was to tell the truth and shame the devil. Canning had neither knowledge nor ability nor strength of will for his post. Hannah was to blot that sentence out, but it has survived. He got into trouble with Wood for cutting down the Madras correspondence with the India Office without authority, and for rashly commenting publicly on a Madras murder case that Madras juries always let off Europeans who murdered Indians. It was not a good case to choose. Wood, on the advice of the Advocate-General, wrote that an English jury would probably not have convicted and urged discretion.

Sir Charles was soon again in dispute with the

Central Government, which rebuked him in terms which he described as such as no public department in England would have addressed to its subordinates. During these months he made no secret of his contempt for the Central Government. In his letters home he entreated Wood to protect the south of India against the incapacity of those who administered affairs at Calcutta. The Central Government tried to do the work of the local governments and paralysed them in the process. It was permeated by the spirit of Bengal and should be transferred to a central place, preferably Delhi. Its functions should be severely curtailed. The Governor-General was away on tour for much of the year and the members of the Council were not up to the job. The Madras men in the Central Government were looked on as foreigners and men of an inferior caste and were discarded if they presumed to voice opinions which did not square with the Bengal standard.

He had some cause for complaint, but he was overdoing it. He sent Wood a letter which he had received from the Central Government, complaining of its captious, sarcastic, insolent tone, but the tone of the letter was plaintive rather than insolent. The Central Government complained, probably with some justification, that the Government of Madras gave no supporting reasons for their opinions and that the Central Government could scarcely suggest a doubt or ask a reason without being accused of wanting to limit the Government of Madras's legitimate freedom of action. It was an old custom that Indian governors carried on direct correspondence with the Secretary of State for India. Wood made no adverse comments on Sir Charles's diatribes. His replies give the impression that he knew Sir Charles was intemperate, but thought him generally in the right. He probably enjoyed sitting in the middle of the controversy.

One matter in which Sir Charles was clearly right

was in his continual advocacy of Delhi as the capital, both from its position and from its historical associations, although, since the days of Curzon, we would hardly subscribe to the argument that it was 'surrounded by immense fields of ruins which would furnish abundant material for new buildings'. The Madras complaint against the north was to continue until the end of the British connection and beyond it, into the argument on the official language which continues to this day. Seventy years after Sir Charles's complaints, the expression 'coming the north over you' was used in Madras to denote an attitude of superiority by the British in the north over their colleagues in the south. There can be little doubt that Sir Charles's defence of Madras's rights against Calcutta was popular in Madras. He wrote to Hannah that the newspapers both in Madras and Calcutta wrote as if he had embarked on an enterprise of extreme peril requiring the greatest audacity. But the real battle was to be on a question of all-India policy.

8

RECALL

J AMES WILSON now comes on the scene, having been appointed the first finance member of the
Governor-General's Council. Wilson had had a varied
career. He had failed in a speculation in indigo, had
become a financial journalist and had founded the
Economist, nearly the whole of which he wrote himself. He was elected to Parliament, was a joint secretary
to the Board of Control and financial secretary to the
Treasury from 1853 to 1857, became Vice-President
of the Board of Trade, Paymaster General and a privy
councillor under Palmerston, and went to India in late
1859 to reform the Indian finances, which were suffering from the effects of the Mutiny. It is clear from Sir
Charles's correspondence that he and Wilson had
quarrelled when they were both at the Treasury.

When Sir Charles heard of the appointment, he
wrote to Hannah that it was a serious matter for him.
He had hoped that he had escaped that trial, but would
try to act wisely. Two months later he was viewing the
prospect more hopefully. He felt that India was big
enough for them both and he would be as courteous and
helpful as possible. He invited Wilson to stay with him
when he passed through Madras, though 'ordering a
salute and giving him a sort of public reception would

be funny'. When Wilson was in Madras, they sparred politely with each other. Wilson tried to get Sir Charles to go to Calcutta for a conference, but Sir Charles replied that he did not wish to leave his province. So they played the opening moves in what was to be a violent contest.

The controversy centred on Wilson's measures to balance the budget. He proposed to introduce income tax, a licence duty on traders and a tax on home-grown tobacco. His general ideas stemmed from Wood's policy, but he acted precipitately and without sufficiently taking into account the views of the men with Indian experience. Sir Charles considered that the way to balance the budget was to reduce military expenditure, and that the proposed taxes were unnecessary and unwise, would arouse bitter opposition and would lead to bureaucratic inquisition and corruption. He saw in Wilson's proposals an intention to maintain an unnecessarily large Indian army which was dangerous in itself, and to make the Indians pay for it. He believed that this policy would lead to disaffection and was based on wrong principles of government. There was much sense in his views, but he wildly overstated them, pouring out a flood of polemical argument, not all of which is convincing and some of which was rank nonsense. Tension between the Central Government and Madras rose until Sir Charles committed a fatal error, which could only lead to his recall. The details of this controversy are now of no interest to more than specialists in Indian economic history, but the human drama still has its own fascination.

John Lawrence wisely warned Sir Charles that there was little honour but much obloquy to be earned by economy and frugality, and that few of our great men had any time for such a policy. Sir Charles argued that internal security was best assured by keeping enough European troops in India and improving the police, strengthened by what were afterwards called military police battalions. This was much safer than having a large Indian army with its own auxiliaries and nothing to do. He was right in this and it was the pattern subsequently adopted throughout India. The argument went on that, if new taxes were to be imposed, they would arouse such opposition that it would not be safe to reduce the army, but that Madras could give the Central Government far more by cutting the army than the new taxes would produce. He unwisely added that it was unfair that Madras, which had remained loyal, should pay for the financial results of the Mutiny, while Bengal was allowed 'to go on its course of unrestrained waste and virtual anarchy'. This was a bad argument, as central taxation could not differentiate between provinces and Sir Charles was not going to help his cause by attacking the Central Government's administration in Bengal.

His argument rested on the claim that he could save money on the army quickly enough to meet the financial crisis and that if he could do this, others could too. Here he had bad luck, of which Wilson took advantage. Wilson told Wood that the Madras military estimates had turned out to be substantially larger than the figure which the Madras Government had given, the mistake having been discovered when the military finance commission visited Madras in December. Sir Charles pointed out that they had corrected the mistake themselves in the previous June, only three weeks after the original figure had been reported, while Wilson had not arrived until November. Oddly enough, Wood repeated Wilson's version to Parliament two months later, as if he had never received Sir Charles's explanation.

Meanwhile, the drama was unfolding. Wilson introduced his financial proposals in the legislative council. Wood wavered. On the same day he congratulated Wilson on his speech, but told him in another letter that he might try reducing the army instead, in spite of the fact that Wilson had already publicly committed himself. Wood twice expressed to Canning his doubts about the new taxes, shared by members of the India Council in London, but left the matter to be decided in Calcutta. He was unable to make up his mind or to intervene effectively. Sir Charles was now in full cry against Wilson. He described the budget as framed with an utter ignorance or recklessness of its applicability to Indian conditions, and the crisis as more important than the Mutiny. He was spoiling his case by his intemperate language, but was supported in more moderate terms by the Governor of Bombay.

The Madras Government sent an open telegram to Calcutta asking that the usual period of three months should be given to receive representations on the bills, implying that they would object. The Central Government rebuked them for not having sent the telegram in cypher. This Sir Charles described as a claim by Wilson to exclusive rights of publicity. On the same day the Central Government wrote to Madras, with a copy to London, that the decision had been taken on their responsibility and that they expected the Madras Government to carry it out. They already had the views of the provincial governments and proposed to suspend standing orders in order to curtail the procedure in the legislature. After further exchanges the Madras Government sent Calcutta and London a long minute objecting to the bills and reported that they had asked the Madras member in the legislative council to advocate their views, lay the papers on the table and move that they be printed. Wilson sent for the Madras member and told him that the Queen's service required that he should not speak in the Council.

At this point, when it was clear that Wilson was going to suppress the Madras Government's views, Sir Charles's old passion for publication became irresistible. Three members of the Madras Council had recorded minutes supporting the Governor's views. Sir Charles, without consulting them, gave the Madras Government's minute and the supporting minutes of the members of his Council to the press, recording that he had done this on his own responsibility in order to secure the greatest possible publicity. The Commander-in-Chief gave his hearty support, but the other members, finding themselves compromised, recorded that Sir Charles had not been justified in publishing their minutes, which were confidential. On the day when the minutes were published, the Central Government sent a telegram to Madras warning the Madras Government against publishing their views, but this telegram could not have arrived before Sir Charles took his action, although he was subsequently accused of having deliberately disobeyed the instruction.

Sir Charles now attacked Wilson personally in his letters to Wood. He wrote that, having acted with Wilson for several years, he knew every inch of him. He had neither religion nor gentlemanly feeling, but only what he thought worldly wisdom. In working out a cherished object of ambition he was utterly unscrupulous. His ambition was to be the English Chancellor of the Exchequer, and, in order to further it, he wanted to make it appear that the finances of India were in a hopeless state and that there was no one in India able to retrieve them until he, the great financial saviour, appeared. To this end the future of India was to be sacrificed. His name was a byword in England as embodying the essence of his selfish egotism. At the same time, Sir Charles lashed out at Canning's 'do-nothing administration'. Ironically, Wilson's wife and daughter were then the Trevelyans' guests, having been rescued by Hannah from their hot rooms in a hotel and lent the Governor's villa by the sea.

Canning was concerned about the effect of Sir Charles's action on the authority of the Central Government. He told Wood that he ought to recall Sir Charles. They could not count on cooperation or discretion from him. He had committed a mischievous folly for the sake of making a splash and bringing himself conspicuously before the public, instead of renewing his representations with the warning that he could not be responsible for the peace and good government of Madras, if Wilson's policy were maintained. That would have put the Central Government in a greater difficulty than that in which they now found themselves. But his head was 'full of wind' and so it would be to the end of the chapter.

Wood, evidently expecting Sir Charles to do something rash, had warned him to be prudent, and that it was contrary to any conceivable mode of carrying on a government that the subordinate parts should publicly declare their opposition to the determination of the chief authority. He hoped that he would not see Lord Canning marching to put down the insurrection of Madras, headed by its Governor, but Sir Charles was running hard upon raising the standard of revolt. But Wood was too late. He had to write recalling Sir Charles, his old friend and colleague. A cabinet had been held, the vote had been unanimous, and its decision was fairer than the administration of so severe a reprimand that Sir Charles could not have remained.

It was a letter full of kindly feeling and genuine sorrow. Wood told of his own misery, remembering their work together in difficult times and their constant friendly intercourse for fourteen years, but he knew that he had only done his duty. He was sorry too on public grounds. Sir Charles had been sometimes irregular towards the Central Government and his colleagues, but had been doing right in the main, and if he had stayed, would have changed the character of the Madras Presidency. He had recorded and would be ready on all occasions to bear testimony to the Government's entire approbation of Sir Charles's general administration. He ended : 'God help you, dear

Trevelyan, and believe me never more than now your sincere friend.'

Wood was much less friendly to Wilson. He wrote that Wilson had not kept them informed of what he was doing and seemed to have been hasty in his calculations. He added that it was a great public misfortune that Sir Charles had made it impossible for him to stay in Madras and that he was personally grieved beyond measure, for Sir Charles was a very old friend and, with all his faults, there was no one for whom he had a greater regard. He wrote to Canning that, however indefensible Sir Charles's conduct had been, a great many people agreed with him and it looked as if Wilson had been run away with by his English notions and by the English community and press in Calcutta. Sir Charles was unrepentant, as usual. He asked Wood to lay all the papers before Parliament and maintained that, once his minute had been suppressed, he had had no alternative but to publish it in order to give time for the issue to be properly considered in London.

Macaulay had died early in the year. Sir Charles paid him an affectionate tribute, as one from whom he had over a long period of years experienced the most generous and consistent kindness. He added that the trial to Hannah, coming as it did in the midst of her distress at leaving home and of her preparations for it, had been a severe one, and he would be thankful when she was safe in Madras. But poor Hannah had arrived with her younger daughter just too late to restrain Sir Charles from taking the fatal step. Their son George said afterwards that it would never have happened if his mother had been there. Now she had to start packing up again. In a letter to Wood, thanking him for his consideration but supporting her husband's position, she mentioned what she described as a curious appendix to the affair. When she had been with Macaulay in the Lakes a few months before his death, Macaulay had asked her to send her husband a message from him; that he believed that Wilson would not rest until he had procured Sir Charles's recall, as the only man in India who could in any way act as a check upon him; that his plan would be to lead Sir Charles on, or to compel him to some act of insubordination, perhaps by use of the press, and that he would then raise the hue and cry for recall. He had sketched exactly what afterwards happened and had begged Sir Charles to take care that the cause and his conduct should be such that he would have a good story to tell when he got home. Hannah had not passed on the message, as she did not want to put ideas into her husband's mind, but she had never doubted what the end would be and was only thankful that he did have a good story to tell.

Sir Charles agreed to leave by the first possible steamer. He declared that his time in Madras had been the most tranquil and prosperous period of his life, a surprising judgement by normal standards, and appeared unconcerned for himself, though he found it sad to see Hannah beginning to pack up again before any of their possessions had been put out. He sent special thanks to Sir Patrick Grant and Bourdillon, his principal supporter among the officials, who afterwards wrote an account of Sir Charles's Madras administration. He took especial care to discourage any expression of feeling which might appear to question the Queen's decision. He received addresses from all communities which, even allowing for the customary tone of such addresses, gave substantial evidence of the respect in which he was held in Madras. The Muslim community particularly thanked him for changing the protocol at Government House and receiving the family of the Nawab of Arcot and many other members of the community. His daughter Alice was just recovering from jaundice, and they had a bad journey home in the hottest part of the year, having to pass three times through the hottest part of the Red Sea, spend some time at Aden and go on in a ship too small for the number of passengers, after the engine of the first ship had broken down.

Wood wrote a decidedly odd letter to Sir H. Ward, the Governor of Ceylon, who was to succeed in Madras. He thought Ward would have no easy task in succeeding Sir Charles, who understood his business and had a heart for the work, but he suspected that Sir Charles had set the people of Madras against him, so that Ward might reap some of the fruits of Sir Charles's unpopularity. He went on to make the absurd statement that Sir Charles had done more to create difficulty in Indian administration than the great rebels of the Mutiny, Nana Sahib and Tantia Topee. Wilson had written to his son-in-law, Walter Bagehot, that many people in Madras said openly that the security obtained by Sir Charles's recall was worth the mischief he had made, and it is possible that Wilson had been giving Wood the same story. Although the members of the Madras Council, whose minutes Sir Charles had published without their consent, had a reasonable cause for complaint against him, it seems more likely that Madras opinion was with him in any quarrel with Calcutta, particularly as it was a question of the imposition of new taxes by Calcutta on Madras without the Madras Government's concurrence.

Wilson was clearly delighted to have got his revenge on his old enemy. He wrote to Bagehot that he thought Sir Charles scarcely accountable for his actions. He had an impulsive and ill-balanced mind, with an overweening confidence in himself, thinking himself able equally to command an army or regenerate the civil government of a country, with a smattering of everything, but profound in nothing, with a dull apprehension, but the most dogged obstinacy he had ever seen, and with an inordinate vanity and love of notoriety to be gratified. Was this just hitting a man when he was down, or was Wilson nervous of what Sir Charles might say when he was back in London?

The most extraordinary aspect of the affair was that this man who had been recalled for insubordination, whom Wood had described as having caused more trouble than the most dangerous rebels, received most flattering eulogies in the House of Commons. Palmerston paid special tribute to his great merits and abilities, to the honesty and integrity of his mind, and to the firmness with which he performed what he considered his duty, regardless of any consequences that might arise to himself. These merits, he said, were too inherent in his character to be overshadowed by this single act, and he looked forward to Sir Charles's further service to his country. Wood spoke of him as a very old personal friend and said that he had never had a more painful duty than in recalling him. Sir Charles published his own statement on his recall and waited until another opportunity for service should occur.

9

INDIA AGAIN

S IR C HARLES did not settle down at home. India
was still his main interest and he asked Wood for
another appointment there or on the India Council.
Wood assured him that he would not be allowed to lie
fallow and in the autumn of 1853 the opportunity
occurred. Wilson had died soon after Sir Charles had
left India. His successor, Laing, had been a failure.
Wood could not find a good man who would take the
post of finance member of the Governor-General's
Council. He offered it to Sir Charles.

It was an extraordinary reversal of circumstances
which Wood had to explain to Lord Elgin, who had
succeeded Canning. He wrote that Sir Charles had all
the qualifications needed. He was a good organiser and
a stern economist. He was pledged to abolish income
tax, which was what Elgin wanted. He was no speaker,
so would not be anxious to become a public figure.
He was a gentleman and independent, not a financier
greedy to make a reputation. He was honest and honourable. To the Queen the appointment was explained
in simple terms. The way in which Sir Charles had
been recalled would prevent his falling into the same
error again. Being in a lower position, he would not
have the same opportunity for insubordination, and the
fact that it was a lower position marked the Govern-

ment's disapproval of the old offence. Delane, the editor of *The Times*, was told that in the old controversy Sir Charles had been much nearer right in substance than anyone had given him credit for. He had been biting the bridle for two years and could now be thoroughly trusted. Wood had found Laing unreliable. He explained his requirement: 'I want a gentleman who will not play tricks.'

Walter Bagehot, perhaps out of loyalty to his father-in-law's memory, devoted a leading article in the *Economist* to his objections to the appointment. What was wanted was a calm man of good judgement. Sir Charles was the reverse of this. He had many eminent qualities, but he was never a safe man; his judgement was not sound; no one could predict what he would do next, whose territory he would invade and trespass on. Sir Charles could afford to take a more kindly view of Wilson than he had in the old days, even if there was some inconsistency involved. He wrote that Wilson was a very able, indefatigable public servant who did much for his country while he lived and ended by sacrificing his life for it after laying the foundation of the new system of Indian finance. There was a certain element of comedy in the situation. Wood sent a copy of Sir Charles's letter to Bagehot.

In the end, Sir Charles had not come too badly out of the Madras affair. Wood told Elgin that Wilson had had the sense to see that he had got himself into a false position. The tobacco tax had never been imposed. The licence tax had been modified and then repealed. The income tax had been modified to exempt lower incomes. No one wanted to keep it on longer than the five years for which it had been imposed, and after that period it was dropped for some years. The dire results which Sir Charles had prophesied had not occurred, but the taxes were not what had originally been proposed and he was proved right in saying that his defiance of the Central Government would not lead to any dire results

either. He had also been proved right in holding
that Indian income was resilient and that expenditure
could be substantially reduced. In three years the military expenditure, about which there had been so much
controversy, was much less and the finances were again
healthy.

When Sir Charles left for India, Wood wrote to
Elgin that he must not mind if Sir Charles was long-
winded. His willing work was cheap at the price. Wood
was, however, still rather nervous how the appointment would turn out. He was soon warning Sir Charles
to take things easily and not to undertake too many
things at once; otherwise he would be sure to create
opposition and difficulties for himself. The warning
was repeated several times. Sir Charles defended himself. It might look as if he was interfering in matters
outside his responsibilities, but, sooner or later, everything was sent to him to be considered from a financial
point of view. He pleaded guilty only to taking on one
small item of work, the Board of Examiners, which
he could have avoided; but the work was play to him;
he did it on Sundays and found it a refreshing change.
His ideas of leisure were very much his own.

The warnings died away as Wood began to have
more confidence that Sir Charles would not do something outrageous. However, Wood gave him some useful advice how to treat Indian subjects at Westminster.
He wrote that the amount of ignorance and nonsense
about Indian matters in the House of Commons was
absurd. Whenever they meddled, it was with some
English view or from some English prejudice, and very
little indeed from knowing anything or caring anything
about Indian interests. It was important therefore to
present to them the recommendations of the Government of India as a whole, and not conflicting opinions
within it.

Sir Charles was a successful finance minister and
there is very little to be said about his last Indian

appointment that could be of interest to the general reader. The last act of Sir Charles's Indian drama was played in low key. His son George, in his life of Macaulay, wrote that the task of interesting Englishmen in the details of Indian administration had baffled every pen except Macaulay's own. I do not propose to try and emulate Macaulay. However, one financial question remains of interest – the attitude to the opium revenue. Wood, like all his family since, was a deeply religious man, but he was not disposed to treat opium as anything but a desirable source of revenue. His only fear was that they depended too much on it, and that it would fall. He was content to leave opium policy to the Government of India, but wanted it dealt with quietly so as not to rouse the 'strict people' by the notion of the Government's encouraging it. It was all nonsense, but it was as well to avoid giving a handle for folly. A year later he made his position even plainer. He wrote that the old moral question was a good deal got over by the legislation on the sale of opium in China. He had never seen much weight in the objection on this score himself and was not afraid of it in Parliament. At the same time he did not want to give any handle to the objectors. However, he would not risk any loss of revenue on this ground.

The finance member, even if he had not been Sir Charles, had to interest himself in frontier policy. In 1863 there was frontier trouble. The Sitana Sayyids (tribal holy men) were harassing the border. The British army mounted an expedition against them, advancing through the Ambela pass with the object of destroying the village of Malka, the Sayyids' local centre, which was more than twenty miles the other side of the pass, in order to discourage them from further attacks on British territory. The column was pinned down on the pass and was continuously attacked by the tribes in fierce fighting, which caused heavy casualties on both sides. After six weeks, it was rein-

forced and moved to the offensive in the valley beyond
the pass. The tribes at last realised that they could not
dislodge the British and gave up the fight. The Buner
tribesmen submitted and agreed to take a small
British party to destroy the Sayyids' village. It was a
hazardous journey, but the tribesmen kept their
promise, the village was burnt and the party returned
safely. The commander of the column, Sir Neville
Chamberlain, having achieved his objective, was able to
retire.

Sir Charles saw this situation from a characteristically
individual point of view. Elgin was at the point of
death. Sir Charles distrusted the Lieutenant Governor,
Sir Robert Montgomery. He had heard that Montgomery wanted to strike a blow to offset the disturbance
to the popular mind in the Punjab caused by a
Mohammedan prophecy that a great event was to take
place in the next year. He argued against a proposal
to give the Commander-in-Chief and the Lieutenant
Governor authority to call up reinforcements, on the
ground that this amounted to an abdication of the
responsibility of the civil Government to decide its
objectives. He was opposed to forward operations,
which he feared might lead to a religious war on
the whole frontier. 'The house is on fire; the master
is lying paralysed; nobody has any authority to act.'
He was contemptuous of the 'English Punjabis', whom
he described as ignorant and wrong-headed. He was
being over-dramatic, but had some arguments on his
side. At one moment the Council ordered the force to
retire. A few days later, to Sir Charles's dismay, the
military men on the Council took the matter into their
own hands, ordered that there should be no retirement
without the Council's express approval, and gave the
Commander-in-Chief authority to organise any force
which might be necessary to support the operations.
But at this point Chamberlain withdrew and the crisis
disappeared as quickly as it had developed.

This was the first time since Akbar's expedition of 1586 that a large force from India had been sent to that part of the border. It was not a good time to initiate a forward policy on the frontier, when there was a power vacuum in Kabul and the Viceroy (as he was now called) was at the point of death. There was good reason to teach the Sitana Sayyids a lesson, but it seems likely that the Punjab Government had seriously under-estimated the resistance which was to be expected and the hazards of a difficult pass, and that the column would have had great difficulty in reaching its objective. Otherwise, it would have moved on to destroy Malka and not have had to take the risk of sending a party under tribal protection to do the job for it. To this extent there were some grounds for Sir Charles's views, but, once the column had been pinned down on the pass a few miles inside tribal territory, the soldiers were probably right in thinking that a retreat which gave the tribes a victory would have had a disastrous effect on the frontier. In the event, after a tough fight and with a bit of luck, the British force was able to retire, having achieved its objective without a large supporting force being required, and the tribes acquired a new respect for the British army, which kept that part of the border quiet until 1897.

Some years before, Sir Charles had given his general views on frontier wars. He considered that there was no symptom of weakness of the central authority so certain in India as the prevalence of obscure, predatory, devastating frontier wars. Metcalfe and Bentinck, in whose school he had been bred, had put an entire stop to them by adopting a just and conciliatory but at the same time firm line of policy, acting upon the interests of these half-civilised warlike tribes and not merely upon their fears. He had read with pain the accounts of the wholesale destruction of life and burning of villages, which made agricultural and pastoral industry and trade impossible.

He developed these views on this occasion. He considered that the Government should not unnecessarily molest the tribes, but should assist their economic development, making it in their interest to be quiet. He argued that it was no good to advance the frontier, because that would only bring the British into connection with wilder and more warlike tribes and lengthen the lines of communication. Coercion should be used where necessary, but the primary policy should be conciliation and mutual interest. There was much sense in what he wrote, but his approach was more convincing in theory than likely to be effective in practice. When John Lawrence became Viceroy, he tried this line on the frontier, but was not very successful.

Sir Charles got on well with Elgin, but he was naturally delighted when, after Elgin's death, his old friend John Lawrence succeeded as Viceroy and Governor-General. He wrote that it was a great comfort to have to do with an earnest and able man, who understood the work and was determined to have it done. The great controversy over the position of the Commander-in-Chief, which reached its height in the tussle between Curzon and Kitchener, was already in being. Wood and Sir Charles both favoured a combination of Commander-in-Chief and Minister of War, Kitchener's thesis, which in the end prevailed, but were unable to persuade John Lawrence, who was surely right. Sir Charles seems to have got on well with the Calcutta businessmen in spite of his continual criticism of the European mercantile community's attitude towards Indians, but it is not surprising that he had to face some attacks. A few months before he left India, Wood wrote about an attack on him in the *Times of India*, which he described as a partial and contemptible performance, advising Sir Charles to cultivate a thick skin and indifference to attacks, as he had.

Wood seemingly showed no distaste for hearing Sir Charles's frank views on his colleagues on the Governor-

General's Council. Sir Charles wrote that Harington was a man of inferior mind. Sir Charles had known him in early life and he had not changed. Out of his judicial line he was narrow-minded, ill-informed and timidly conservative. Grey was deeply imbued with service feeling and was averse to any changes which invaded the established Anglo-Indian routine. He could not believe that so able a man could be so prejudiced, but it was a fact; it was *esprit de corps*. Maine was as liberally disposed as he could be, but he knew nothing of India. Napier had turned out to be a very incapable civilian administrator. He was honourable, well-disposed and not without a certain sort of balancing common sense, but he was entirely ignorant of civil affairs and was of an over-cautious, hesitating nature, which quite unfitted him for his place. Sir Charles added that he remained on perfectly good terms with all his colleagues; he had resolved not to quarrel and had learned to take things as they came and to make the best of them. He would not have been on such good terms with his colleagues if they had known what he was writing about them to Wood.

In 1863 Hannah and the children spent some months in the Nilgiris. Judging by his letters, Sir Charles was more relaxed than at any time in his Indian career. He thanked his wife and daughter for their devotion during the depressing two years of 'forced, discredited inaction', rejoiced in Wood's approval of his first budget, and even indulged in a little mild irony in his comment that Prince Albert's speeches read like the life of Christ, only with less human nature, the most perfect men not always being the most amusing. The family did not have good health and as early as the summer of 1863 Sir Charles had written that he would not remain long in India. Wood did his best to induce him to stay, at any rate until he had finished his work on the currency, the accounts and the general financial arrangements of India. He had hoped to see his third budget through, but he fell ill again and left India in April 1865.

He had stayed long enough to restore his reputation after the disaster of 1860. Throughout these last Indian years Wood had showed great confidence in him. He told Sir Charles that he could entirely and thoroughly rely on him and that he did not know anybody else who could be so thoroughly trusted on every Indian subject. He felt really happy to have been able to place Sir Charles in a position of so much usefulness. He would not regret having returned to India.

Sir Charles could not have wished for a more generous appreciation of his services. He had fully justified himself. Yet, in this so cordial relationship between these two men, there was a slight jar at the end. After all those expressions of confidence over many months, Sir Charles ended by proposing financial measures with which Wood wholly disagreed. In June, Wood wrote to India that he had had a great deal of conversation on the question with Sir Charles on his return, but could not say that he was much the wiser. So ended their long association in England and in India, not free from difficulties and misunderstandings, interrupted by one cataclysmic event, but concluding in peace and harmony with only a faint echo of a false note.

10

FATHER AND SON

During his last two periods of service in India, Sir Charles, with his immense energy, had found time to give his views to Wood on every conceivable question of Indian policy in frequent letters of great length in his own clear hand, apologising on the rare occasions when the pressure of work compelled him to use an 'amanuensis'. Time and again he reverted to the question of the Government's policy towards Christianity. After the Mutiny there were strong pressures in favour of the Government's taking a more active part in the work of conversion. It was a very British form of Christianity, when an Indian congregation was required to join in prayers for the Queen, the royal family, the clergy and Parliament, and an observer was brought to wonder what the congregation lisping the words 'Victoria and Albert' made of it all. For some earnest Christians it also had strong Old Testament overtones. We read of the author of an account of scenes of Anglo-Indian life visiting a village, seeing the priest on the threshold of his temple, wishing for the fire-compelling hand of Elijah and wondering when the cup of the vengeance of the Most High would run over.

Sir Charles, who himself believed that Christianity was the greatest benefit that the British could confer on

Indians, never wavered from his old view that its advancement must depend on voluntary effort and that the Government must make it clear that they had no intention of interfering with local religions. A district official in Madras had ordered the markets in his district to be closed on Sundays. This, he declared, was an extraordinary instance of that folly and bigotry from which misunderstandings were likely to arise in India as to the intentions and the fair dealing of the Government on the subject of religion. He was concerned also with the example set by the European society and soldiery, for the improvement of which spiritual instruction was necessary, given by able chaplains who had their hearts in their work. The religion of the British in India was essentially evangelical and no High Church chaplains should be sent to India. That piece of advice might well have been given seventy years later.

He was greatly concerned about the relations between the communities. While he was in Madras, discharged men of the 1st Fusiliers had killed three Mohammedans at Arcot to the cry of Cawnpore and Lucknow. In dealing with the case his aim was to impress on both parties that impartial justice would be done, since confidence in the Government was 'the last anchor'. When he returned to Calcutta, he was more than ever concerned by the deterioration in relations between Europeans and Indians which had occurred since the Mutiny. He recalled that when he was a young man in Calcutta, all the top people were engaged in education and other work for the benefit of the Indians. When he returned twenty-five years later, he found that no one cared any more for that sort of work and no one learned Indian languages unless he had to. Wood told him that he was not surprised at hearing this, having also been told that the estrangement between the communities was going lower among the Indians and higher among the Europeans.

Sir Charles had always had the lowest opinion of the

European indigo planters. He had written to Wood that it was the most difficult thing in the world to get it out of the heads of Europeans that they had a right to the labour of the Indians, and that they suffered a wrong when that labour was not made available on the terms which they approved. There had been substance in this view, for Wood had written to Canning about a proposal by the planters to re-enact a regulation which had been repealed twenty-five years before, which would make breaches of contract a criminal offence. His view was that as indigo cultivation was practically forced labour, the Government could not pass strong enactments to compel its performance. Now, four years later, Sir Charles wrote that the entire mercantile and planting interests were intent on securing a position of advantage over the Indians quite beyond the situation in former days.

He looked forward to increasing participation of Indians in Government and the civil administration, including membership of provincial councils, and was continually producing schemes of constitutional reform with this end in view. He had a respect for the Indian officials and even looked forward to Indians holding commissioned rank in the army – hardly a proposal likely to find general approval in those days after the Mutiny.

Sir Charles was naturally concerned to observe the way in which the new class of Indian civil servants, recruited by competitive examination, were turning out in practice. He thought that the new method of selection had proved a decided success. After all the criticisms to which they had been subjected, the worst imputations against them were that they were not fond of society and field sports and that their manners were not good. As a class they were cultivated, thoughtful and intelligent, and keen on their work. Most of them had the finish of public school and college life, but some of them, although good men and likely to do well in

the end, had suddenly been brought out of obscure
corners of society and therefore suffered from deficiencies in their bringing-up and education. This tendency
was aggravated by the grant of £100 for their expenses,
which subsidised candidates from what he called the
pupil-teacher class. No special favour should be shown
to the rich, but wealth ought to be allowed its just influence as an element of cultivation and refinement.
The civil service of India ought not to be filled at the
public expense with 'sizars and servitors'. The Indians
were emphatically gentlemen and did not like to have
other than gentlemen to rule over them. Reform in
the mid-century had its proper limits.

He was far from being an imperialist. As Governor
of Madras he was ready to spare troops for the China
war from the south, but was relieved that the British
Government did not contemplate a major campaign
against the Chinese emperor. He described the world
scene as an age of unjust wars and believed the public
had become so corrupted that they hardly stopped to
reflect on the evils of war or to consider whether a war
was just or necessary, or not. The Afghan war had led
the dance and then came Sind, Gwalior, the second
Burmese and the first Chinese war, and, at the time he
wrote, we were, in his belief, more completely in the
wrong in China than ever. He regarded the policy of
the annexation of Indian states before the Mutiny as
being 'near relation to this precious brood', though that
hardly squared with his views on Mysore.

In 1863 his son George joined him for a time as un-
paid private secretary. In later life George Otto Trevelyan belonged, in the words of his son and biographer,
to a type that flourished most in the reign of Queen
Victoria : the literary man who was also a politician, the
politician and literary man who was also an historian.
He was already a considerable intellectual and literary
figure at Harrow, having swept up all the school prizes,
won the English prize poem three years running, and

produced topical English verse in imitation of Juvenal. At Cambridge he read and re-read the classical authors for pleasure, down to the most obscure, was placed second in the Tripos, and in his spare time produced elegant satirical verse, including the often quoted description of the undergraduate dinner in hall, which annoyed Whewell, the Master of Trinity:

> We still consume, with mingled shame and grief,
> Veal that is tottering on the verge of beef.

His father had written from Madras for his Harrow and Cambridge verse, but was not allowed to have it until he promised that he would not publish it. George knew his father's habits only too well.

Though no athlete, he always took vigorous exercise and hunted with the Prince of Wales, with whom he became friendly when they were both up at Trinity. He failed twice to get a fellowship, the second time in company with Jebb, since fellowships were then given by seniority. It was a waste of time to go on trying; so he gave up his academic career and decided to join his father in India.

On his way out, this formidable young man was still writing light verse:

> Fair dames, whose easy chairs in goodly row
> Fringe either bulwark of the P & O;
> Whose guardian angels with auspicious gales
> Swell the broad bosom of our outward sails,
> Or, as a metaphor more strictly true,
> Direct the revolutions of our screw;
> As the long day wears on, and nothing brings
> To break the dull monotony of things,
> No fresh delight, no genial Christmas fun
> Save water-ices or a casual bun,
> Just like our watches, as we Eastward go,
> We're growing slower still and yet more slow.

He was not the man to make less than full use of his opportunities. He travelled round India and wrote a series of letters on British life in the country, which were published anonymously in Macmillan's magazine, and republished in 1864 under his own name, while his father was still in India, as a collection under the title *The Competition Wallah*. These lively letters were still being reprinted over forty years after the original edition. He was obviously to some extent influenced by his father's views, but the letters were a very individual production and he made up his own mind on the basis of first-hand impressions.

In the preface to the book he wrote that the earlier letters about the Indian Civilian's life had been taken to be written by a 'civilian' with a predilection for his own service. That was of little consequence; but not so with a later letter, which, in his words, exposed at length the horrible tone adopted by a certain class of Englishman in India regarding the murder of Indians by Europeans. He explained that though it consisted almost entirely of extracts from the British Press in India, it was called by *The Spectator* 'a burst of civilian hatred against the independent settler'. He had also been described by *The Spectator* as prejudiced against the settlers on the evidence of another letter attacking the proposed Criminal Contract Law, for which the settlers were still pressing, though the facts in the letter had been drawn almost entirely from the writings of advocates of the law.

He explained how his own opinions had gradually changed as a result of study and travel in India. He entreated his critics to show that he was wrong in his facts; that the European settlers cherished a kindly feeling towards the cultivators; that they spoke of them as equals in the eyes of the law; that they did not call them niggers and treat them as such; that they did not regard as execrable hypocrisy the sentiment that we held India for the benefit of the inhabitants. He claimed that the letters would not have been written in vain if, by their means, Indians obtained some portion of sympathy and English justice. Sir Charles had wisely stopped writing for the press during the tenure of his post as Member of Council; but the family tradition was maintained, and it was not surprising if some of the criticism rubbed off against George's father during his last months in Calcutta.

George had no doubt that the Indian Civil Service was a fine career, which held out splendid prospects to honourable ambition. But better far than this, there was no career which so surely inspired men with the desire to do something useful in their generation; to leave their mark upon the world for good, and not for evil. It was, he wrote, a rare phenomenon this, of a race of statesmen and judges scattered throughout a conquered land, ruling it not with an eye to private profit, not even in the selfish interests of the mother country, but in single-minded solicitude for the happiness and improvement of the inhabitants.

He was able to see the British through the eyes of the Indian peasant. As he described it, the peculiar qualities which mark the Englishmen were singularly distasteful to the Oriental and were sure to be strangely distorted when seen from his point of view. We were regarded by our Eastern subjects as a species of quaint and somewhat objectionable demons, with a rare aptitude for fighting and administration; foul and degraded in our habits, though not to be judged by the same standard as ordinary men; not malevolent (at least the official fiends), but wayward and unaccountable; a race of demi-devils; neither quite human, nor quite supernatural, who had been settled in the country by the will of fate and seemed very much inclined to stay there by their own.

He recognised that India was not going to be converted to Christianity and discussed the reasons. One was the superiority of modern Christianity. The early

English had been converted for the practical benefits which they got out of it. The missionaries had failed to give up the European type of life. Conversion brought adverse social consequences. It did not help that one class of our countrymen called the converts Christian brothers, so long as another class persisted in calling them damned niggers. Lastly, there was the weakening of Christianity by science, which affected educated Indians. Our business was principally to educate, enlighten and fight against superstition, and he fell back on the thought that it was the same God who could be approached by different ways, a point which many earnest Christians in India have since reached.

Of the events during the Mutiny in Cawnpore he wrote a separate account a year later, which was still being reprinted in 1910. He condemned both the mutineers' savagery and the excesses of British vengeance and did not hesitate to tell the truth. He wrote that from the lowest depths of our nature emerged those sombre, ill-omened instincts, of whose very existence we had ceased to be aware. It was tacitly acknowledged that mercy, charity, the dignity and sacredness of human life, must be put aside. It was well that nations, as men, should be delivered from temptation. With the grim determination and the dogged pertinacity of our race, men went forth over the face of the land to shoot and sabre and hang and blow from guns till the work should be accomplished. He put it to the credit of the 'civilians' that they listened to the voice of equity and humanity and did not allow the impressions left by the events of the Mutiny to influence their opinions and their conduct, but the case was very different with the settlers. It was a bitter indictment of their conduct towards Indians, especially when an Englishman was brought to account for outrage or oppression. Why, he asked, is an Indian always 'polished off' and an Englishman 'publicly strangled'?

Even in those days Calcutta was an unlovely city.

The place was so bad by nature, he wrote, that human efforts could do little to make it worse; but that little had been done faithfully and assiduously. God made the country, evidently without a view to its becoming a European colony, and man made the town, and the Municipal Council made the drains. At Barrackpur, he continued, where the average rate of mortality did not much exceed that in the Irish quarter of Liverpool during a typhus epidemic, the air appeared balmy and genial to a visitor from the capital, in the hateful climate of which the mental faculties degenerated surely and rapidly. Everything pointed to his father's solution, to move the capital into the interior of upper India.

Neither father nor son saw India again. George Trevelyan embarked on his political career. Sir Charles Trevelyan was made a baronet for his services and lived until the age of seventy-nine, having married again in his later years after Hannah's death. I end this account of his Indian career and opinions as I began, by quoting George Macaulay Trevelyan, his grandson:

Once more I recall him in his strong old age as squire of Wallington, with his tall, wiry frame, his snow-white hair, his face as rugged as a sea-worn rock, its deep lines instinct with energy and power, the eyes alive for every happening. Though always talking or brooding over some scheme of improvement, he was kind and uncensorious in the ordinary ways of life. His evangelicalism had by that time become an attitude of the soul rather than a dogmatic creed; at least it was tempered by reason and good sense, and by wide reading conducted on plans originally suggested to him by Macaulay.

Whatever Charles Trevelyan's faults, his roughness of character, his lack of humour and tolerance, his determination and courage, his single-minded struggle for his principles, gave him a quality of greatness. The members of his family and Englishmen in general may be proud that he once represented Britain in India. Indians who cherished his memory for so long, will recognise in him one of those many Englishmen who tried to deal decently with them and to do their duty, as they saw it, for the benefit of India.

The Trevelyans built a church at Cambo, up the hill from Wallington, Charles's home in his old age. Here on a windy Northumbrian hill he is buried. He is commemorated in a window in the tower which he built, by the saying of St Paul, so appropriate to his life; 'I have fought a good fight; I have finished my course.'

TWILIGHT OF EMPIRE
1929-47

I

THE LAST BRITISH
GENERATION

T H E years passed and the setting changed. The last
generation of British in India faced political problems
very different from those of Charles Trevelyan's time.
The Indian empire was near its end. For over a hundred years the British services had been honest and
efficient, if sometimes unimaginative. Their members
had maintained firmly but justly the twin pillars of
Indian administration – law and order and the revenue. They had brought new ways of farming to the
countryside and had irrigated vast tracts of barren land.
They had built good roads and railways, encouraged
private industry and freed the country from its old sub-
servience to British commercial interests. They had
begun to spread electric power and had preserved and
increased the wealth of the forests. They had created a
fine medical service and transformed public health.
They had developed a system of higher education approaching western standards, though it had become
overweighted on the side of literature and law, and the
development of the national culture and languages had
lagged behind. They had not kept the administration
in their own hands. At the end, there were only just
over five hundred British members of the Indian Civil

Service; the technical services, engineering, forest, medical, education, were almost wholly manned by Indians. In the countryside very few British faces were to be seen. There were still few Indian senior officers in the army, but even there the change from British to Indian was gathering pace.

In the course of his career, an Indian civilian might find himself anything from High Court judge to Resident in the Persian Gulf; from president of a port trust to guardian to a maharaja; but basically he was a revenue officer. India was and, whatever the strength of its industry, always will be a country of peasants. The revenue was mainly derived from the land. The prosperity of the countryside depended on a sound revenue administration, on the assurance in the minds of the peasants that they would be treated fairly and that their essential needs were understood and met. Generations of Englishmen had spent their lives in painstaking, unseen work in the Indian villages, assessing and collecting the revenue and granting remission for failure of crops, giving loans for the purchase of seed or implements or for digging wells, settling land disputes, persuading the peasant to improve his methods of farming, the health of his family, the condition of his house, his village and his cattle, and listening, always listening, to petitions on a multitude of little matters which were of vital importance to the life of those patient, hard-working, undernourished people.

It was easy to mock the Englishman in India. His limitations were obvious, his social prejudices stupid. In England he was looked on as the prize specimen of the middle class. The English music-hall proclaimed that 'The men who live in Poona would infinitely sooner play single-handed polo, a sort of solo polo, than play a single chukka with a chap who isn't pukka.' No one in England was interested in the problems of an Indian district, nor in the least impressed by the achievements of these worthy, conscientious people who so seldom settled happily into the life of their own country after retirement and whose thoughts never left their old life.

It was easy to abuse them, and visiting left-wing politicians assured their Indian audiences that the Englishmen in India did not represent their countrymen at home. But they deserved neither mockery nor abuse. Nor did they indulge in self-pity. They enjoyed life. In spite of the discomforts, the exhausting climate, the absence of the arts, which the English rarely miss, the separation for long periods from their country and their family, the 'Indian civilians' lived a full and satisfying life. They had continuous and serious responsibility, independence and authority, an outdoor life, plenty of sport and devoted servants. They did not envy their old university friends in the home civil service on the 8.45 a.m. train from Sevenoaks.

The British in India adapted their habits of life to the climate and were more influenced by Indian attitudes and customs than they perhaps realised. Their servants put them into their clothes and addressed them as 'protector of the poor', just as if they were serving an Indian master. They changed for dinner in the jungle not in order to assert their social superiority over the Indians, but for the practical reason that in the climate of the plains they had sweated all day into their clothes. The Indians too changed their clothes in the evenings. In the country districts of the south, they had tea and bread and butter at dawn, rode for an hour or so, took their breakfast at ten o'clock and spent from eleven to five in the office. It was the Indian timetable. Their addiction to protocol and ceremony was wholly in accord with Indian ideas.

The official caste system was rigidly maintained by British and Indians. The Indian Civil Service, the ambition of every Indian father for his son, came first, then the other imperial services, then the provincial administrative service. Each official had his allotted niche and, with the help of the warrant of precedence, there could be no doubt of the relative position of an assistant superintendent of police in the C.I.D. and the deputy director of an ordnance factory. Protocol had its comic side, as usual. A very superior general from the Brigade of Guards observed with some heat at Government House, Ootacamund, 'I cannot help thinking that these people who go into dinner ahead of me are the wretched people who put up little bungalows round my place in Hampshire.' Businessmen, however rich, were a lesser breed than the mandarins of the civil service; 'box-wallahs', as they were contemptuously called. Among them there was a clear dividing line. Those who sold by the ton were respectable; those who sold by the pound were not accepted in society or the clubs. The whole elaborate system was an amalgam of British class and Indian caste.

In British India the clubs were the centre of British masculine social life. Almost all rigorously excluded Indians, even as guests. In the cities women were excluded from the main buildings, but provided for in annexes, as in some London clubs. In the Madras club the women were not allowed to watch the men playing tennis and, if they transgressed, were warned off by the Madrassi boys in their white linen hats with wide brims and sweeping skirts, recalling the old prints of Madras life. In the country clubs the women were allowed into the main buildings, but not normally admitted to the bar, and, even today, in these half-deserted clubs, now having mainly Indian members, the old notices are still there, 'women not admitted beyond this point', while within the sanctum only a row of empty high stools waits for the ghosts of dead planters to order their gin and bitters in the oppressive pall of the noonday heat.

Lord Willingdon had tried, in Bombay and Madras, to get Indians admitted to the British clubs; but not even the initiative of a popular Governor, not other-

wise suspected of liberal tendencies, sufficed to break
the old habits. He could only turn the flank of the old
guard by founding new clubs in Delhi and Bombay.
Some reason might be found in national membership
in a city where there were exclusive Indian clubs, but
for keeping out Indian guests there was no justification
whatsoever. The clubs did more than anything else to
bring the British community into disrepute in India
and at home.

The clubs kept their old ways until independence
forced a change. As late as the spring of 1947 the sub-
scription library in a hill-station in northern India still
displayed a notice that it was reserved for Europeans
and Anglo-Indians. Books were to be for the white and
the half-white only. In Bangalore cantonment the Indians could bathe their brown bodies in the swimming-
pool and dance with the English girls, since the cantonment was in the Mysore State, but even Indian officers
with the king's commission were not allowed to vote
at the club meetings and the combined efforts of the
resident and the general commanding the district were
not strong enough to get the rules changed. A Maharaja might be a friend of the King and a member of the
'Squadron', but not allowed to enter the club a few
miles outside the borders of his State or the yacht club
in Bombay. The segregationist argued that the Indian
wanted to belong to a mixed club, but kept his wife
or wives in purdah. However, the friendly relations
between British and Indians in the mixed clubs in the
States and in the clubs founded by the Willingdons
effectively rebutted the diehards' arguments, though
this did not change their views.

The two communities, British and Indian, met on
their official and commercial business and on social
occasions with an official flavour, but otherwise pursued
their own separate ways, with their different habits and
outlook on life, treating each other with toleration;
the British doing their duty as they saw it, preserving

the old order as a matter of course, but admitting some gradual change; the Indians accepting the British framework of their lives and seeming to be hardly disturbing themselves with the thought that, through the pressures of a changing world, they were soon to receive the satisfactions and discomforts of independence. In a large part of the country the political struggle hardly ruffled the surface until the end of British rule was in sight, when the machine began to run down and communal passions could no longer be kept in check. Only the professional politicians were active in opposition to British rule and even their leaders still looked for so much to England, thought in British terms and sent their sons to get the best English education that they could afford.

It seemed in those days a relatively settled society; yet behind it, with its powerful apparatus for maintaining law and order, the scene was dominated by Gandhi, half saint, half politician, who, by the power of his ideas and his shrewd understanding of his own people, hastened the end of British rule. The British found Gandhi an exasperating negotiator, with whom it was impossible to reach a firm agreement. Nor did Indians bestow on him an uncritical adulation. A prominent congressman from Madras told me that he and his colleagues respected Gandhi's aims, but did not trust his methods. The political leader whom they most admired was Rajendra Prasad, later President of India. Gandhi's fasts against his own people were unsuccessful. His asceticism, however genuinely an expression of his beliefs, was calculated for its political effect. A whole third-class coach was reserved for him on the railways; a throng of disciples and goats followed him wherever he went, and Mrs Sarojini Naidu's witticism about the cost of keeping the old man in poverty has passed into history.

Gandhi's achievement was in the development of a successful political weapon, non-cooperation, admirably adapted to a fight against a foreign government which had overwhelming physical strength, but which was markedly susceptible to the moral pressure of its own liberal tradition and world opinion. He attacked the British at their weakest point. He was a brilliant publicist and became the symbol of the new India for most Hindus and some Muslims, and for innumerable sympathisers outside India. The Gandhi cap and the home-spun cloth, *khaddar*, became the symbol of political respectability. He had a shrewd instinct for the real good of the Indian peasant and was not misled by an exaggerated expectation of the benefits to be derived from industrialisation. He was a social reformer as well as a politician, notably in his sustained campaign against the age-long oppression of the 'depressed classes' by the caste Hindus. He never ceased his efforts to achieve communal harmony and he died for this principle. He was mourned by the millions who revered him, though, if he had lived, he would have become an ever sharper thorn in the flesh of the Congress leaders who had inherited the fruits of his life of struggle.

Indian independence was not won solely by a fight against the foreign occupier. The British, who had acquired their Indian empire as a practical requirement for successful trading, were never wholehearted imperialists in India. The vision of the generation of Charles Trevelyan's youth, pursuing policies which they knew would lead to independence, was blurred in later years, but never wholly lost, and the increasingly insistent demands of the Congress party, being based on the liberal principles inculcated by the British masters, received the sympathy and sometimes even the active support of sections of British public opinion. In the twentieth century, political life in India was part struggle, part negotiation, first between British and Indians and, as independence approached, between British, Congress and the Muslim League under Jinnah. It was never a struggle to the death with the

British, though it nearly became one between Hindu and Muslim, and, in the end, independence was achieved by peaceful agreement with the British without a serious weakening of the administration, except in the areas affected by the worst of the communal conflict, where there was a bloody prelude to the establishment of the two independent states carved out of the old India.

In the last years of British rule, it was clear that the time for decision had come. The fatal antipathy between the communities, which had not been created by the British but was deeply embedded in Indian history, could only be resolved by a settlement imposed by the British and by their simultaneous disappearance from the scene. The Indians who served the British remained loyal to their service under all the physical and spiritual pressures imposed on them by the nationalist revolution, which could not but touch their hearts. Even at the height of the most violent manifestations of 'non-violent' civil disobedience during the war, the Government's machine was strong enough to contain the Congress revolt. We knew that if India could have been isolated from world opinion, if the British people had had the will to stay, they could have stayed for some time. But we knew also that they would not. The will to empire was no longer there. The relative power of the British in the world was declining. Once they had started down the steep slope of withdrawal, they could neither retrace their steps nor pause on the way. And, whatever contrary currents had swept the generations succeeding those great Englishmen of the early part of the nineteenth century, however strong the baleful effect of the Mutiny on British thought and attitudes, the old beliefs and aims were still our beliefs and aims. Our purpose was still to bring the country to independence in peace. The time had come for Indians to govern themselves and to give a new stimulus to economic development and social reform. So in those last years our real, our almost impossible task was to find a way to leave, as soon as the overriding necessities of war had been met.

2

A YOUNG MADRAS 'CIVILIAN'

O n 29 November 1929 the *Viceroy of India* deposited me in Bombay. I was just twenty-four. My first impression was of a near-naked labourer carrying a heavy burden on his head, walking past an enormous advertisement for an American refrigerator. It was the essence of the Indian problem. So many were hungry, while the West forged ahead.

I took the train to Madras. In my first week there I was welcomed in the homes of my Indian friends and saw how British and Indians were separated into social compartments, overlapping but never fusing. Was it really the same world which I had left? Everything was different – the heat, the glare, the smells, the noises, the houses, the furniture, the food. I thought, I don't like this at all, and felt a little sick.

They told me I was to go to Coimbatore as assistant collector for training under the collector, the principal revenue officer and magistrate of the 'district'. It was an ugly little town in the dusty plain under the Nilgiri hills, the pattern of an Anglo-Indian country 'station' with all its parochialism and prejudices exhibited in the British club in which, with rare exceptions, no Indians, other than the servants, were allowed to set foot. Around the town sprawled the sandy villages with the houses of the principal landowner, the money-lender and the village official built of brick, the rest of dried earth with roofs of palm leaves, each with its compound full of goats, buffaloes and dogs, the doorstep embellished by the women with intricate chalk patterns every morning. Each village had its little crudely painted temples, poor descendants of the great Buddhist stupas, the communal well, a great banyan tree spreading its sacred tendrils and providing a meeting place for the village assembly, and little stone reliefs of Hanuman the monkey god or Ganesh the pot-bellied elephant-headed god who brings you luck. Round every village, behind every hedge, was accumulated the natural consequences of the absence of any form of sanitation and of the daily habit of the villagers of going for a walk with a purpose at dawn. It was not surprising that the land immediately surrounding a village was the most fertile and valuable.

I was keen to work, to improve my knowledge of Tamil, to get to know and understand my new Indian surroundings. I was told only to get to know the 'station'. I had come straight from Berlin and the Alps. The shock was severe. I was rude, precocious, arrogant and insecure, unwilling to adjust myself to my new surroundings or to understand that this little British community, however limited their outlook, were doing their jobs ably and conscientiously. I fought against my new life; I thought of giving up and going home. I stayed at home and read, when I should have been at the club. I climbed the nearest outcrop of the Nilgiris, fell down a steep slope and nearly killed myself. I made no allowance for the deep differences in the social habits of British and Indians. But I still think I was right. It was a petty, narrow community, based on official position and colour, the most rigid defenders of the social barriers being the families of mixed descent or with generations of life in India who had lost their English roots and who, in order to conceal their own Indian origins or associations, despised everything Indian and asserted their rights as members of an exclusive caste.

I found relief in learning Tamil from my clerk, a little, weak-bodied Brahmin who shaved his face and head together once a week, wore the old-fashioned bun on the nape of the neck and dressed in shirt and dhoti, the cloth girded round the waist, hanging down to the ankles and looped between the legs. He told me how he had climbed on pilgrimage to a neighbouring shrine, two steps forward and one back, holding in his mouth, like Papageno in *The Magic Flute*, an instrument preventing speech, which he offered to the god after taking the ceremonial bath. His mother had been possessed of a devil. The priest drew a circle round her at night, chanting his holy charms, demanding the name of the spirit, beating her continually, until in the morning the spirit gave in and told his name. Then the force went out of him, he left the body and the woman fell down senseless. It was Jacob wrestling with the angel.

The new collector was a man of intelligence and sympathy. He quickly saw what was wrong and sent me to report on a primitive tribe living in a malarial tract between two ranges of high hills, sharing it with a unique herd of white bison. Walking with these primitive people in single file through the forest, I saw for the first time how the outcastes could get their drinking water only from the channels which had irrigated the fields of the caste villagers. Perhaps after all it was worth staying in India if one could help to improve a few people's lives.

I was soon summoned to Ootacamund, the summer headquarters of the Madras Government in the Nilgiri hills, where Hannah Trevelyan and her children had spent the summer of 1863. As Emily Eden had found, it is an exhilarating experience to drive up the hillside from the heat of the plains to the sharp air of the high plateau and the pungent smell of the eucalyptus trees. Here life was more stimulating. At least, it was a progression from the suburbs to the shires, to the meets of the Ooty hounds and the society of intelligent Indians and English in the Madras Government. My task was simple – to decipher telegrams from the Government of India which were coming in at great speed during the civil disobedience movement. I had to receive the immediate telegrams in the middle of the night. But I learned from experience that none of them were in the least urgent and, with the full agreement of my superiors, I used to leave them unopened until morning. I became so expert at signing for them in my sleep that I used to wake up in the morning and look with curiosity at my bedside table to see how many I had signed for in the course of the night. So I learned one of the basic facts of Indian life, 'Delhi is far away', as the old Indian proverb went, and saw how those exceedingly competent men who were the Government of Madras looked with an indulgent or irritated sense of superiority on the antics of the men at the centre who busied themselves sending unnecessary immediate telegrams and did not understand the south.

Ootacamund in 1930 was not very different from what it had been when Macaulay visited it, though the English official society had been diluted by the planters and the atmosphere was more sporting and less intellectual than in the days when Macaulay's copy of *Clarissa Harlowe* was passed eagerly from hand to hand. It was only an hour's journey down to those teeming Indian villages on the plains; yet it might have been in a different country. Even the indigenous inhabitants, the Todas, with their curious beehive temples, whose origins were uncertain, seemed to have no links with the Tamils below. It was like one of those mysterious isolated plateaux discovered by Rider Haggard's heroes in the heart of Africa, ruled over by a beautiful white queen, though here it turned out to be a fair representation of an English county, with society dominated by the great county family in Government House on the hill.

The place really belonged to the planters, extravagant and vivid characters, who had hacked their way
through the jungle to a fortune, rather than to the
officials taking temporary refuge from the heat of the
plains. The working planters lived sober, hard-working,
open-air lives on their estates, invading Ooty once a
year for their annual saturnalia, known as planters'
week. With the Ooty hounds, the golf courses, the races
and the broad expanse of downs, the place encouraged
a relaxation of the social and political restraints of life
below. Indians and British mixed more freely and a
Congress politician who had arranged not to be in gaol
during his annual holiday in the hills, could be seen
drinking his whisky at the golf-club.

The most talented lady in the Ootacamund of those
days, was the wife of a judge, who wrote novels of
Anglo-Indian life. Her brother, a member of the Indian
police, had been killed in an ambush in a revolt of the
primitive tribes who lived in wild hilly country in the
interior, halfway between Madras and Calcutta. She
said that he had fallen into the clutches of a bank
manager's wife, who had secured a hold over him by an
adroit mixture of religion and sex, which ended with
his paying the lady's bills. The judge's wife took her
revenge, portraying the lady in a novel with bitter in-
cisiveness. In Ootacamund she was living in a house
with two sets of rooms. She occupied the one, in the
other was the lady in the case. It could have been a
Kipling story. The judge's wife, a shrewd observer of
Anglo-Indian life, said: 'We are accused of immorality.
How can we live immoral lives in houses with no doors
and with servants who walk on bare feet?'

Later in the year, the new entrants into the Indian
Civil Service who had been posted to the Madras Presidency were collected in camp near Madras for revenue
survey training. Two of them married in breach of caste
rules, which remained a strong social sanction. One
marriage, for which I acted as a witness, was performed

by a Brahmin convert to theosophy, since it was an inter-caste marriage, virtually unknown at that time. The other was between the wrong kind of cousins, with the father's brother's daughter, not, as it should have been, with the 'cross cousin', the father's sister's or the mother's brother's daughter, the favoured type of marriage among the matrilineal Nairs of Malabar. The bridegroom's father told me that he had allowed the marriage against strong family objections, since there could be no physiological basis for the old custom. We later became friends with a brilliant Indian painter married, fortunately happily, according to the rules of their caste, to her mother's brother. These old customs presumably stemmed largely from the wish to keep the property in the family.

Indians in the civil service were often from humble families. I have dined in a small district headquarters with a judge whose cook was the collector's brother-in-law. It seemed to be taken quite naturally, without embarrassment. The clever son of a Brahmin clerk was able, without resources, to get a degree from the Madras university, pass into the civil service and go to England for two years' training at Government expense. On the auspicious day the boy would leave his strict vegetarian home for a hotel until the ship sailed, unless by a lucky chance the ship's sailing date fitted with the Hindu calendar. He would take his first nervous step into the outer world by boarding a P & O liner in the second class, where he would find a menu consisting largely of roast beef, forbidden to the Hindu, with no concession to the religion or tastes of the inhabitants of the country from which the P & O derived a large slice of its income. On return he might strive to appear so Western in his habits that he became almost a caricature of a young Englishman, but that I have found to be more common further east.

The intelligent young Indian, often of a subtle intelligence, was more likely to wish to emphasise his

separateness from the English. One in camp with us did
so by inviting us to watch him eat in the Brahmin manner the food cooked for him alone by his Brahmin cook,
as he sat on the ground, half naked, dressed only in the
dhoti and the Brahmanical thread.

Another young Brahmin with us in camp was of ex-
ceptionally independent character, neither submitting
to his caste rules, nor aping Western manners. He had
even refused to submit to the sacred thread ceremony
at puberty, virtually a denial of his Brahmin status. I
wrote an account of the tragedy which ensued, which
has survived these forty years:

Saturday. We have now been for a week in this
deserted cantonment. The name Poonamalee is said
to be an English corruption of a much more beautiful
Tamil name, Puvirunthamali, meaning the hill of
flowers. It hardly lives up to its name, but near my
tent is a frangipani tree, with white flowers and a
stupefying scent, the only suggestion I have found
of the Orient of the romances. We live close together
in tents and the air is full of contrasting patterns of
sound, representing the different ways of Indians and
English amusing themselves. From one corner comes
the smack of golf club on ball as we English play
our games. From another corner pours out the high-
pitched gabble, the sudden scream of laughter of
the south Indian talking English, probably an in-
consequent mixture of philosophical subtleties and
jokes which, as Aldous Huxley wrote, would have
sounded old-fashioned in a preparatory school.

I had not met him before this camp. He is a Tamil
Brahmin; his father is a man with a great reputation
in the public service; he is highly sophisticated with,
I think, a first-class brain. He is by no means one-
sided. He is a philosopher, a reasonable hockey-
player, a born conversationalist and has managed to
absorb a greater range of European culture in the

comparatively short time that he was in Europe than any other Indian I have met. He knows his French literature, he has travelled and observed with intelligence in Germany, France and Italy, he has some knowledge of European music, he has known people in the intellectual and social worlds. But his main characteristic seems to be an almost obstinate independence. He refuses at present to marry. I can already see what courage that requires in his circumstances. He is reserved and difficult in his manner and surprisingly uneffusive for a south Indian.

He has now decided to buy a horse. It is, I suppose, a matter of self-respect. Englishmen own horses; so he must at least have had one. Coming back from a game of hockey yesterday, he told me about his purchase, but would not tell me where he had got his horse. I think I understand. For his own satisfaction – some would call it vanity – the enterprise must be completely his own. A very interesting character. I have talked a lot to him lately, but it is an acquaintanceship which cannot be forced, especially as I am an Englishman in India; it must come naturally. This bar of different foods is a serious hindrance. I think he will do well in his job, as he is immensely keen on it and on the country, and his mind is not overweighted on the academic side.

Sunday. This morning I was woken up by the sound of running feet and shouting. His head had hit a coconut tree after the horse had run away with him; the leg and skull were fractured. Warren, who is in charge of the camp, took him into Madras. He was unconscious. We had our breakfast thinking that we would not see him for another few months. To tea with Sankara. His house has the inevitable three trade calendars, a kitchen clock and pictures which could fortunately only be seen if one were strung up by a pulley to the ceiling. I no longer find this disconcerting, since I am beginning to regard it as part of the atmosphere of hospitable and agreeable simplicity which I feel at once in so many of these houses, though I still received a shock at seeing an oleograph of crude catholic design in his own room. Here we learned of the seriousness of the accident and motored together to the hospital. We inquired of an aged attendant the way to the European Officers' ward (shades of the past) and told him whom we wanted to see. He replied cheerfully, as if at the successful termination of a difficult job: 'Why, he's dead; he's in the mortuary.'

Tuesday. The funeral is to be tomorrow, when his father comes. To me the strange aspect of the affair is the unresting curiosity about every detail of the death, the preservation of the body and the funeral arrangements, which seems to come naturally to all his Indian friends. This emotional curiosity of the East is perhaps due to the nearness of the processes of life and death in this country, from which the West has fenced itself off with a barrier of mechanical and mental systems of sanitation.

Wednesday. I arrived late at the hospital. In the afternoon heat, in a small yard, faced by ugly windowless walls on one side and on the other by a distant view of a busy town street, there stood a featureless building, the mortuary. Round it were gathered a large heterogeneous crowd waiting idly. A few cars stood in the middle. The eager curiosity, the avid interest in details continued. 'Come on, let's keep together – they've got a permit to keep the body on ice for more than twenty-four hours – there is the father ... the mother ... the younger brother ...' The father came out of the mortuary, a grey-haired elderly man, with a face of brilliant and kindly quality. He was in European clothes and was led away to change his clothes, seeming only half-conscious of his surroundings. The friends and relations pressed into the mortuary to view the body and the sightseers clung to the shutters and peered through the chinks. The crowd grew denser as a fresh batch, for no apparent reason, were let in by the gate which gave onto the street. My friends came out; 'Terrible, terrible; so swollen, you know; you could not recognise him. You see, the difficulty is to take him off the ice, as he has been there for three days. They are putting him on the bier now . . .'

The female relations now came out, among them three widows dressed in white, looking like three witches, carrying their little pots and knowing that at last they had him in their power. And indeed they had. That independent spirit who had refused marriage and the sacred thread ceremony, cynical, agnostic, was now brought unresisting into the power of the oppressive orthodoxy from which he had broken free, and the thread which, alive, he had refused, they tied upon him in death. The women – strange beings to me, symbols of that real Indian life which I shall never be able to know, and without knowing which one cannot really know Indians – all crowded into the cars; woman after woman piling onto the back seat of an American car and even onto the floor, under the order of a voluble male relation who appeared to recognise fully the importance of his position as a kind of master of ceremonies. The old father came out, dressed now in a dhoti, using a cheap bazaar towel stamped with the maker's name in red letters, as an upper cloth, yet remaining a dignified figure. The cars moved off, and, carried on a rough bier out of the mortuary, came the body, covered by a white cloth up to the shoulders, leaving the head open to view – a great head, unrecognisable, swollen, shaven, smeared with white, showing the scars of the wounds and lolling slowly, helplessly at the swing of the bearers' stride, as they passed into the street.

Thursday. His tents were taken down and all evidence of his presence had gone. This morning the noise of hammering made me look up from a lecture to see the tents going slowly up again. It seems they were taken down without authorisation, and now a somewhat ghoulish reconstruction is taking place, for the father is coming this evening ...

He came. A large crowd followed him to the spot; every Indian friend of his son waited for an opportunity to present themselves and follow too. Ananthanarayanan says, Indians do not leave each other alone in matters of the emotions. So the father and mother visited the bloodstained tree, surrounded by a crowd of two or three hundred. It has been a bad year for the parents. They tell me that last year one daughter's husband died. She is therefore, as a Hindu widow, bound to an existence in which she will be a nonentity for the rest of her life. The other daughter was seriously ill. I was told afterwards; 'He bore it well, very well.'

Friday. Today all traces are again cleared away. A last echo is in the *Madras Mail*: 'Death's iron hand has cast upon the parents a thick heavy gloom by removing one nearest and dearest to them. It is with the deepest sorrow that one contemplates the end of the bright career just begun. Respect for elders was bred in his bone. He was one of those who practised the team spirit among his mates ...' He would have got a malicious enjoyment reading it.

Charles Trevelyan
at the Treasury.
Engraving by F.
Joubert from the
painting by
E. U. Eddis.

In old age.

Hannah More
Macaulay Trevelyan.

Sir Charles Wood
by George Richmond.
By permission of
the Earl of Halifax.

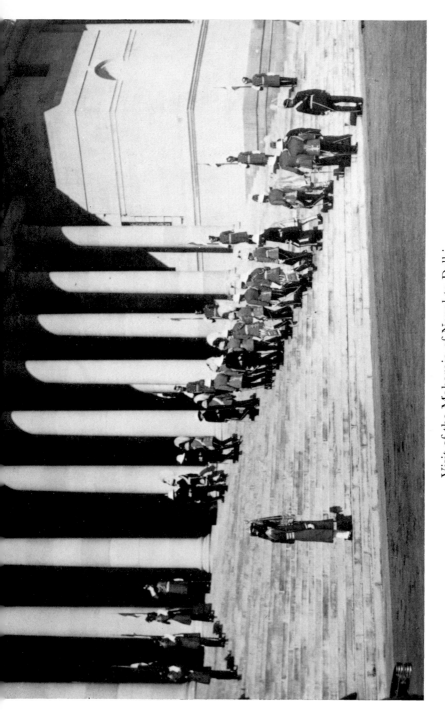

Visit of the Maharaja of Nepal to Delhi.

Above
Kheddah in Mysore.

Below
Procession in Mysore.

Procession on the
lake at Udaipur.

The palace at Udaipur.

Above

The author with the
Maharaja of Chhatarpur.

Below

Installation of the
Maharaja of Chhatarpur.

Charkhari:
By the lake.

Charkhari:
Ceremonial salute.

Presenting the first Chinese
Ambassador to India, 1947.

Parting present from
Jawaharlal Nehru.

Jawaharlal Nehru
June 1947

3

THE BRITISH IN THE SOUTH

THE south was littered with the memorials of the Europeans who had spent their lives there during the past three hundred years; the old cantonments with their mouldering barracks and disused handball courts, the coastal forts, the British Fort St George in Madras, which still contained the secretariat of the Madras Government, the Dutch fort at Sadras, with its seventeenth-century tombstones bearing the arms of the deceased elaborately carved in granite, the Danish in Tranquebar, the French in Mahé and Pondicherry. The French were still there. Their energies were largely devoted to repelling spiritual and physical encroachments by the perfidious British. Disputes over the smallest alleged encroachments flourished. In shocked tones the French Governor protested that coolies of the public works department had dug a channel through a little island formed from silt at the mouth of the Godaveri river, thus committing the heinous crime of causing a piece of French territory totally to disappear.

The classical and baroque churches had settled happily into the landscape, the gothic looked out of place and uncomfortable in the tropical sun away from the northern mists. The most striking memorials of the past were the spacious eighteenth-century merchants' houses in Madras. These classical mansions were perfectly fitted to the merchants' lavish way of life, pompous, yet elegant and practical, with their deep verandahs, rows of columns and black and white marble floors, standing in compounds of fifteen acres or more of park land studded with great banyan trees, each house with its 'bibikhana' for the merchants' girls and with a dark lower floor where the owner could take refuge in the hottest days of the damp Madras summer. They had altered little since the time of William Hickey, though Victorian manners had banished the girls to the squalid brothels in the city.

In the days of the East India Company, the collector of a district in the Madras Presidency had been a kind of English Raja, remaining for many years in one place, subject to only intermittent control by his distant superiors, living more an Indian than a European life, ruling his district personally in a manner agreeable to Indian traditions and displaying the Raja's characteristic virtues and vices. His power and prestige was much greater than that of his twentieth-century successors, but he was apt to get into trouble from mixing up his official and personal finances. The last vestiges of the old lax system were eradicated by Charles Trevelyan during his period as governor. It had to go, but some good was lost in the process.

Among the men of the old type was Rouse Peter, for sixteen years collector of Madura, who had died in debt to the Treasury to the amount of seven lakhs of rupees, but was probably well worth it. He was remembered in his district a hundred years later as Peter Pandya, being honoured with the name of the ancient local dynasty. There was Mr Snodgrass, collector of Ganjam. Word reached him that inspectors from the Board of Revenue were coming to examine his accounts. He welcomed them cordially in his summer-house on the edge of the Chilka lake, but gave them some sad news. He had been anxious to put some finishing touches to his accounts and had taken them with him for his afternoon row on the lake. A sudden squall had got up, the boat had overturned, he had scarcely escaped with his life and his precious accounts were at the bottom of the lake. The inspectors were unsympathetic and Mr Snodgrass, dismissed without pension, had to be dislodged from his district by force. Back in England, he was still full of fight. Every day he set out in a carriage and pair for Leadenhall street, dressed in rags and provided with a banner recording the monstrous injustice of his dismissal without pension after thirty-five years in the company's service. The moral pressure on the directors was too strong. They gave way.

There was the collector who, hearing of the impending visit of an inspector, had him waylaid and robbed and then appeared in the nick of time to rescue him and thus earn his gratitude, a device afterwards favoured by P. G. Wodehouse's heroes. There was the inspector who deliberately let it be known that he was on his way to examine the accounts of a collector who was conducting a flourishing money-lending business with official funds, in order that, when he arrived, he should find all the outstanding loans back in the Treasury. There seems to have been a perpetual contest of wits between the English Rajas and their official superiors at Madras. These were typical of the stories current in my time about our predecessors of a century before, those little monarchs in their lonely kingdoms, absolute masters of their districts and to be reached only with difficulty by ship, horse or bullock cart.

These conditions of life bred eccentrics too, who flourished up to the last generation. One collector asked the Board of Revenue for permission to take his mother into camp, omitting to add that she was dead and embalmed and that he kept her in his office over the protests of the Brahmin lawyers. Another invited the local society to a grand party in his garden to witness his wife's cremation; a third confirmed his reputation for inefficiency by trying to burn his wife's corpse on a hill road with green wood in the rain. One would not allow his gardener to use the garden shears except in gloves; another, whom I knew, brilliant and erratic, teased the Government by writing his fortnightly reports in verse. The ghosts were, of course, strictly British, including the carriages which drove up to the Collector's house in Tanjore on the same day every year, and dear old Mrs Moberley, who had died some years before in Ootacamund and confused the household by ringing the bells and passing through people while they were dressing.

The general standard of Madras 'civilians' when I went to India was high. The best were very good indeed, including the High Court judges such as Sir d'Arcy Reilly, whom I have heard dictate a decision in open court in an exceedingly complicated case, without reserving judgement, in forty minutes of pellucid English, without hesitation or correction; or Sir Gilbert Jackson, a notable classical scholar, who neatly summed up the changing attitude of the 'civilians' in the verse:

> Efficiency, a flame, no less
> The older men allowed
> To guide them through the wilderness;
> But we, a lesser breed, confess
> To sympathy, a cloud.

Brodie castle, the most imaginative of the merchants' palaces in Madras, with its long drawing-room jutting out over the Adyar river and catching every breeze, was occupied in 1930 by Charles Cotton, then Chief Secretary to the Madras Government, who had furnished it with a fine collection of eighteenth-century furniture and china made in or for south India, and the Daniel brothers' paintings and prints of local scenes. He was typical of the old school of 'civilians' who had served for long periods in Malabar. His servants were part of the family. One had become so powerful while Cotton was Resident in Travancore State,

that the Government of India had taken the unprece-
dented step of insisting on his dismissal, but the man's
son was still living in the house and being educated at
Cotton's expense. When I was staying with Cotton, to
whom I was related, the current major-domo was
acquiring something of the same position. I remember
well the scene one morning as the great man, a spruce
little figure in his white topee, silk suit, monocle and
Old Etonian tie, emerged on the steps of the portico,
while his car and attendants waited below. At his right
hand was the major-domo. A petition was presented,
doubtless at a cost of one rupee to the servants. The
great man took it and handed it to his servant, saying,
'What shall we do with this?' The major-domo read it
and replied, 'We should send it to the Board of Revenue.' The great man stepped into his car. The peti-
tioner was probably entirely satisfied. The procedure
was in accord with Indian custom. Bureaucracy had not
been allowed to destroy the personal touch.

Another famous member of the 'Malabar school' was
the brilliant Loftus Tottenham, an old man as I remember him, who was reputed to have progeny all down
the west coast and whose attachment to the attractive
Malayali women was implicit in his saying that the
Tamil woman was God's answer to the prayer, Lead
us not into temptation. Retirement in England was
torture to him. He returned to south India to be Chief
Minister of a little State, where he died happily in
office. In his favourite posture, cross-legged on a stool,
looking like Alice's caterpillar in the Tenniel drawing,
he presented an odd figure. But he was one of the best
of the old type of Madras civil servant, more effective
than some of the latter-day bureaucrats, unimpeach-
able in their morals, expert at handling files, but without human sympathy and so without the personal
influence of the older breed.

For some months I was attached to the Secretariat in
Madras. English society in Madras was still Victorian

in habits and atmosphere. At the beginning of the century the young 'civilian' had been required to put on a morning-coat and drive in his buggy round the great houses in the heat of the day between noon and two o'clock to pay his formal calls in person. In 1930 we were spared that, but still had to take a taxi and visit all the houses on the list, putting the prescribed number of cards in the tin boxes at their gates. It was an exhausting undertaking, since Madras city extended for about ten miles and the taxi drivers went on the principle that it was not good policy to confess to total ignorance where any of the houses were and that it was better to try the first likely looking house and hope that luck had brought you to the right one. Not to call was a major crime; calling entailed obligatory attendance at a dinner-party at which you were required to eat a formidable array of courses likely to end with a savoury followed by one or even two puddings, in company with fellow-guests normally incompatible with one another and apparently selected from the callers' list by drawing names out of a hat.

That at least was the suggestion whispered to me by a member of the Governor's council with whom I lodged in one of the mansions near the Adyar river, as we went down to dinner to face the prospect of a more than usually unpromising bunch of guests. He had recently married a young and determined lady, with many admirable qualities, but with a touch of the sergeant-major. She had inherited, along with energy and initiative, all the wild temper of her grandmother, the famous Honoria Lawrence, wife of Sir Henry Lawrence, who was killed while defending the Residency at Lucknow during the Mutiny. On Sunday mornings the washerman was received with a stream of imprecations which greatly impressed the household, while her husband and I kept our heads down, emerging cautiously when the storm was over. Her terms of abuse were considered proper to her status. Abuse among the Tamil

servants was devoted either to the exact degree of incest
committed by the other protagonist or to an assessment
of the extent of his impotence, perhaps illustrated by
reference to the appropriate time as shown by the hands
of a clock. She could scream at him that he was a bloody
fool and no one minded. If she had said that he was
useless, he would have marched off.

It was necessary to learn the local meanings of apparently harmless English words. Two young men came to
Madras to a textile firm. One used the foul language
that he had learned at home. The workers did not mind
in the least. The other, a mild young man, never swore.
He went no further than to call a man a rascal. There
was an uproar; it was a deadly insult. The word had
acquired some obscene esoteric meaning in the Tamil
mind. English politicians were apt to forget in the
atmosphere of Westminster that their comments on
Indian affairs would be closely scrutinised in India and
that the metaphors should be inoffensive to Indian ears.
Sir Samuel Hoare, notably sympathetic to Indian political aspirations, was not forgiven in India for having
used the phrase, 'The dogs bark, but the caravan passes
on.'

The Tamil names had been too much for the British,
who had converted Tirunelveli into Tinnivelly, Kan-
chipuram into Conjeeveram, Tanjavur into Tanjore.
The most curious adventure in nomenclature had been
suffered by one of the Madras bridges, originally named
after its architect, Hamilton. The Tamils pronounced
it 'ambattan', the Tamil word for 'barber'; so it got
retranslated and became 'Barber's bridge'. The Indian
city had been called 'Blacktown' in the eighteenth century, but was prudently altered to 'Georgetown', being
by the side of Fort St George. The English spoke the
Dravidian languages badly. The south Indians spoke
English very well, some better than most Englishmen,
even if it did occasionally sound more like Burke or
Macaulay than current speech.

There were some special local variants. 'Quite' meant 'very', which you had to know when a reporting officer wrote that a man's work was 'quite good'. 'Rather very' meant 'exceedingly', one degree stronger than 'very', not one degree weaker as one might have expected. 'V.E.' on a file meant 'very emergent', a logical adjectival form of the word 'emergency' current in eighteenth-century English. A word might become suspect from the derogatory overtones with which it was used. 'Eurasian' became 'Anglo-Indian'; 'Asiatic' became 'Asian'; 'native' could be used of the English in England, but not of the Indians in India. 'Vernacular' had to go, when someone pointed out that by derivation it meant 'slave language'. The English used enough Indian words to make a dictionary of them. It is a fascinating sport to pursue their derivations. In south India a bed was a cot. Was this a corruption of the Portuguese 'catre'? Was the term 'boy' derived from the 'Boyans', a depressed class which provided many of the servants during the eighteenth century?

Occasionally, a perfectly logical use of English sounded comic to English ears, as when a nervous young doctor, summoned to see the formidable Lady Chetwode, said to her staff officer, 'I have examined Her Excellency's front side; have I your permission to examine Her Excellency's backside?' There were obvious errors of association, as when a magistrate wrote a judgement for me acquitting the accused on the ground that the Corpus Christi could not be found. But the retailers of 'babuisms' were often the Englishmen who had not taken the trouble to learn the local language. I have no doubt that the Romans took much the same attitude towards the provincial Latin of the Spanish, the Gauls and the Britons. We have chosen to spread our language round the world and must accept that the English dialects of Madras, Texas, Tokyo, Lagos and Oxford now have equal validity.

*   *   *

There was one institution in Madras which did not conform to Indian or British pattern. By the Adyar river, separated by the river from the British houses, was the headquarters of the theosophical movement. I paid one visit of curiosity to the theosophists to hear Annie Besant discoursing to the faithful under the famous banyan tree. The movement had nearly come to grief in its first conjuring trick phase, when messages from the 'great white brothers of Tibet', allegedly written on rice paper bought in Kashmir by Madame Blavatsky's friend, Colonel Olcott, had appeared mysteriously to the faithful in a niche in an upstairs room of the old house which, according to unkind critics, communicated with Madame Blavatsky's room next door. At the moment of danger, Annie Besant had taken over the movement and purged it of its more ridiculous semi-magical accretions, concentrating attention on its theistic doctrines.

I wandered in and attached myself to the listening crowd. Mrs Besant was having difficulty in answering the questions of a Czech poet, so naïve as to be unanswerable except in the most trite fashion. He asked her, 'Do you consider it better to be good and not a bit clever, or clever and not a bit good?' She quickly diverted the conversation to what was clearly a favourite theme, the iniquity of private property, relating how she had given a friendly welcome to a young thief who had designs on her belongings. I reflected that it is easy to disbelieve in private property if the faithful, including rich American ladies floating round Adyar in wisps of tulle, provide one with a comfortable home, servants and all the requirements of life, including a Rolls-Royce, chauffeur and petrol.

I had no desire to get sucked into official life in Madras. My aim was to transfer to the Political Department of the Government of India. It was better that I should spend my time in the south with an independent charge in the country, until the Political Department should have a vacancy. I was happy to return to the post of sub-collector in the Dindigul division of the Madura district, which I had already held for some months. After this interlude, I did no more than pass through Madras until I revisited it in 1968.

4

THE TAMIL COUNTRYSIDE

THE collector of a district was also district magistrate. He was responsible for order, was in general control of the police and, with his subordinate magistrates, administered the criminal law. Indians, brought up on English liberal theories about the separation of powers, criticised the system, but it worked well. The magistrates did not unduly favour the police, but they did not forget that they, with the police, were responsible for keeping the peace. Violence was never far below the surface in the Indian countryside and the average citizen knew that a firm hand was necessary.

The sessions judge bore a heavy burden in this teeming Tamil country, full of murder, riot and violence, with its endless civil disputes over family property and inheritance. The standard of the judges was high and, though some English judges might be unconsciously biased in favour of the police and some Indian judges in favour of the accused, the people had confidence that they would get justice. The difference between British and Indian judges in their handling of the criminal law was a matter of temperament. The British inclined to robust common-sense; the Indians, with their subtle minds, explored nice distinctions of law and judicial precedent. Both, in my experience, were impartial and completely honest. Murderers were hanged, though it was arguable whether hanging was a deterrent in a community in which a convicted murderer refused to appeal on the ground that he had not yet finished with his victim, who would get too long a start on him in the next world if he were not hanged quickly. In Madura, for a time, no murderer was hanged, since the wife of the Brahmin judge was pregnant and the judge feared an evil spell on the unborn son. The acquittal of many murderers was due to the skill of an English barrister practising all over the southern districts. When he visited Coimbatore for a case, a crowd of ex-clients who owed their life to him, expressed their gratitude by sitting silently for hours on the verandah outside his room in the club, in order to greet him respectfully as he passed.

The British civil law, admirable in so many ways, put a brake on social reform, since the judgements of the High Court were inevitably based on a recognition of the Hindu social customs, and gave added weight to all the inequalities and injustices which they embodied. The criminal law was based on the Indian Penal Code, which owed so much to Macaulay's work as law member of the Governor-General's council, when Charles Trevelyan lived with him. It was admirably suited to Indian conditions and had become a part of Indian life. In the north a heavy iron-shod club, with which a murder could be committed, was known as a '302' stick, section 302 of the code being the section for murder, and so on down the scale to the '323' stick, a light bamboo, capable of inflicting only simple hurt.

A hundred years before, Munro in Madras and Elphinstone in Bombay had tried to found criminal justice on the village assembly known as the panchayat and Sleeman in the central provinces had strongly criticised the failure of the British system to use the Indian institutions and to recognise that their sanctions were far more highly respected than the new procedure and the new oath. It was a plausible view, but I doubt whether it was possible to marry the two systems. The Indian system could only be accepted as a whole with much of what in our view was gross injustice, and my own experience of the latter-day attempts to use the village panchayats in minor criminal cases was not encouraging.

Dindigul was a small country town in the plains, dominated by a fort built on an outcrop of the Palni hills. Local society consisted of two Dutchmen making cigars, an Anglo-Indian police officer and the Indian lawyers. They used to meet at their club in the evenings for a highly unusual game of bridge. The spectators took part, criticising freely during the playing of the hand. If the man whose turn it was to play hesitated, a hand would appear over his shoulder, pluck out a card and lead it. When I was first appointed to Dindigul I was just twenty-five, thrown out on my own and therefore happy, for I was working all day and every day at a fascinating job.

I could escape from the heat of the plains to my duties in the cool of the Palni hills, which included being responsible for the Maharaja of Nabha, a small State in the Punjab, who was detained in Kodaikanal for his sins, and walking a hundred miles in a week inspecting forest land which the owners wanted to clear for the cultivation of bananas and cardamon, our interest being the protection of the catchment area. In the lower malarial hills the villages had musical names, Bodinaikanur, Arasappapillaipatti, Kulikachettipatti. Among the visitors to Kodaikanal was the old ex-President of Congress, C. Vijayaraghavachariar, reputed to be the oldest living ex-political prisoner, whose family, as I have related, still remembered Sir Charles Trevelyan as a notable liberal Governor of Madras. It was the height of Gandhi's first big campaign of civil disobedience. To the scandal of the British residents, I used to row round the lake with the old man and his grandson, both of them clad in *khaddar* and Gandhi caps. British and Indians were never real enemies, for all the outward struggle.

I heard criminal cases all day long. The first accused was a woman suckling her child. I convicted an Indian priest for setting a mantrap in the woods round the jesuit college near Kodaikanal. I gave prison sentences to the young Congress workers who tried to disrupt the train services by pulling the communication cord and had the decisions reversed on appeal, on the ground that the railway company advertised that the penalty was a fine. I tried to protect the villagers from the various ingenious frauds practised on them. The poor people could never resist the alchemist, who gave so convincing a demonstration of his powers by turning one gold coin into two and hopped out of the back window as soon as his victim had been induced to part with his store. The villagers rioted, stabbed each other and cut off a nose if a young man had gone too far with one of the girls. The village houses were an invitation to burglars. There were the cases in which the man was clearly guilty, but the evidence not good enough, or in which the man was clearly guilty and the evidence good but probably false. It was worrying when you felt sure that the man was innocent and the evidence false, but there was no reason on the evidence to acquit.

The Tamil police inspectors, particularly the Brahmins, were mostly able men, but not too scrupulous in their methods. One could not blame them too much. They had a rough people to deal with and many Indian magistrates would not convict on circumstantial evidence, which forced the police to manufacture eye-witnesses. A rich man would buy the prosecution witnesses. The police would retaliate by concocting new evidence and, if they knew they could not get a conviction, 'dragged' him, as it was called, through the courts up to the High Court, knowing that it would cost him a great deal in lawyers' fees to get off. They would 'frame' an enemy and were not above a little

blackmail, but they were astonishingly loyal, steadfast
and efficient in difficult times, and it was they who
really kept the peace.

The police were continually attacked by the Congress
party, which accused them of inflicting a variety of
tortures on members of the party. They treated these
attacks with indifference, so long as the Government
supported them and did not give way to demands for
inquiries into their conduct, whenever they were required to suppress a riot. The Government rightly
refused to give way except in the most exceptional circumstances, for it would have been impossible to keep
order if police facing a rioting mob were reluctant to
act for fear of a subsequent political inquiry. In 1969
the Indian press in Bengal was full of the same kind
of fulminations as in the old days, except that they were
against the Congress Government instead of the British,
and in 1969 the provincial Government was supporting
a general strike, the police did not dare to act without a
written authorisation by a minister and anyone who
took his car out of the garage had it smashed.

The accusations of the Congress party against the
police had some substance. When I was working in the
Madras secretariat in between two periods at Dindigul,
the members of the Madras Assembly were putting
questions every day about police action against Congress demonstrators. The Government invariably
answered with complete sincerity after local inquiry
that the allegations were untrue. Most of the ques-
tioners alleged that demonstrators were beaten in police
stations. I discussed the matter, on my return to Dindigul, with the Anglo-Indian deputy superintendent
of police. I can recall almost his exact words: 'Do you
mean to say that the Government believe what they
say in the Assembly? Of course we beat these people in
the police stations. They are only town roughs hired
by the Congress party. If we were to beat them in the
streets, which we are legally entitled to do, people

would be very upset. They would not like to see it. Everyone knows that they are beaten in the police stations and everyone approves.' What could I reply? I could only say that I could not sanction any action not allowed by law: but I knew that nothing I said would make any difference and that if they changed their methods, the outcry in the Assembly would be much worse.

The methods used by the police to deal with demonstrators lying down in front of the trams were ingenious. In Lucknow the police put down their backs those noxious caterpillars which leave a weal on the skin as they walk over it. Sikander Mirza, later President of Pakistan, when deputy commissioner of Peshawar, noticed that the demonstrators took a tea-break every morning. So he paid the tea-seller to put a strong dose in the tea. The demonstrators drank their tea and lay down again in front of the trams. In a few minutes they had scuttled for home and did not return. The Congress leaders naturally took full advantage of the difficulties of a foreign Government with a tradition of free speech and free political action. We knew that the Government of independent India would use much stronger methods and that for the Congress the enjoyable luxury of putting the Government and the police in the wrong for keeping order would not survive the disappearance of the British. And so it turned out. All the old methods of keeping order were retained and reinforced, and, if one is to believe stories now current in India, police methods have by no means improved.

In the countryside the peace was kept by the use of the legal machinery to impose a social stigma on the malefactor who was too clever to be caught, or the village factions who had to be prevented from murdering each other. The Criminal Procedure Code enabled the police to ask a magistrate to bind a man over to be of good behaviour for a year or two under security, which would be forfeited if he was convicted of an offence in that period. This was especially used to deal with the village magnate who used agents to commit his crimes, could bribe the witnesses and could therefore never be caught himself. There was little likelihood of the authorities being able to forfeit the security and one would have expected the man to have continued his career of crime with impunity. But to be known as a '107 man', this being the section of the code used, was to be branded as a bad man and the procedure was surprisingly effective. Many a village riot was prevented in the same way. The problem of the big man who used others to commit his crimes was one of the most difficult with which the police had to deal. One of the favourite activities of these racketeers was a very localised crime, which required a special section of the Indian Penal Code. It was known as 'clue-hire'. A man could be convicted for receiving money as a consideration for arranging for the return of stolen property, generally cattle. In almost every case, he had first had the cattle stolen, though this could not be proved.

One such case put me in an awkward situation. It became clear to me, while the evidence for the prosecution was being given, that I should not be able to convict on it since, whatever the truth of the alleged facts, the evidence was demonstrably false. By acquitting the accused, I should be taking a different view of the facts from that taken by the sessions court which had had to consider the same evidence in an allied case and had convicted the accused. At that point, I was visited by Bertie Ffoulkes, the only English land-owner in the district, who was enmeshed in local politics. He said that his people had a request which he had promised to pass on to me without comment. Would I delay the case until a certain local election was over? I did my best to hurry the case on. While it was still being heard, I received an anonymous letter, presumably from the man's political opponents, accusing me of betraying the principles of British justice by arranging to acquit the

accused against the evidence, at Ffoulkes's request. I
was saved from having to acquit him by being transferred to another district. That had nothing to do with
this case, though they said locally that it had. I was
living alone, thinking of nothing but the work. I have
not forgotten how deeply this disturbed me at the time.

A German adventurer had made a fortune in south
India at the end of the eighteenth century as an 'inter-
loper' in the days of the Company's trading monopoly.
One of his descendants had married into a good Muslim
family of Hyderabad and their daughter had married
Ffoulkes's father, a chaplain on the Madras establishment. Their sons lived on the family estates. Bertie
lived in Madura, partly with the British, partly with
the Indian community, and was close to Hindus and
Muslims in a way which no transient Englishman could
hope to emulate. One day after dinner he produced a
party of Muslim devotees of a local saint, who gave a
performance in honour of the saint and to earn their
living. The drummers beat out a complicated rhythm,
while the rest of the party stuck long needles through
their cheeks and the flesh of the stomach. There was
no bleeding, except a little from a small boy, presumably a cadet under training. They took heavy spikes
and gouged out their eyeballs and, after some encouragement and much drumming, banged a spike into
a young man's skull, showing us at close quarters the
spike sticking in his head and the hole after one of them
had pulled it out with a jerk, bracing his leg against the
man's shoulder. No one seemed any the worse for it.

Ffoulkes played a prominent part by hereditary right
in the Chhitirai festival. Apart from Benares, Madura
is the most Hindu city in India. It is dominated by the
great temple, with its many courtyards, halls and towers,
every inch filled with a profusion of plaster gods and
goddesses. For the festival, which was held in the height
of summer, a temporary temple was built in the dry
bed of the river. On the first day the Kallars, a local

tribe who were probably descended from the original Dravidian inhabitants of the locality, big strong men with a notable criminal record, placed their God Alagarswami on a litter and brought him from his temple in the hills some distance away, in procession to Madura. He was held in special veneration by the Kallars, who invoked his aid when setting out on a robbery and gave him part of the proceeds. During the night before the festival began, the God rested on the outskirts of the city and in the morning approached the river by a road lined by open stone pavilions, carved like a Hindu temple. A hundred thousand pilgrims gathered in the river-bed and on the ceremonial way. The God rested in each pavilion on his way and the owners of each of his temporary resting-places gave him offerings and fed their quota, some hundreds of Brahmins. One pavilion belonged to Bertie Ffoulkes, who performed his obligations punctiliously. He invited us to meet the God, a little figure riding a horse, with ruby and gold stirrups given to him a hundred years before by the famous old collector, Rouse Peter, and a ruby and gold belt given by Ffoulkes. He carried a boomerang and club, the Kallars' traditional weapons. According to local tradition, he insisted on being bathed only in the water of a cool, clear stream which flowed above his temple in the hills, and turned black with displeasure if he was bathed in any other water. In my memory, he certainly had a black face, like the dark, Dravidian Kallars who carried him. He rested with us for a few minutes, while the priests attending on him on his litter bound scarves round our heads, and then passed on his way.

The god's purpose, repeated every year, was to visit his sister, Meenakshi, who lived in the great Madura temple. The story that I heard was that on arriving at the river, he learned, to his fury and dismay, that the Brahmins had married her to Siva. He therefore refused to go further and stayed for a few days in temporary quarters in the dry river-bed, until he left on his return to his home in the hills. The version in the *Gazetteer* is that he arrived too late for the wedding. I prefer the first version which suggests that this ceremony reflected the impact of Aryan Brahminism on the Dravidian religions of the south.

Relics of the old cults survived. There was still snake-worship in Malabar. The smallpox goddess, Mariyamma, was still propitiated in the Tamil villages. A passover ceremony was held annually in her honour in the village of Bhavani in the Coimbatore district. Every household sacrificed a goat on their doorstep to ward off smallpox during the coming year. In this ceremony Mariyamma was carried in procession on a fine litter of ivory and wood given by another of the early English collectors, who had left his name on it and was still remembered in the district after a hundred years for his benefactions and for having got into trouble with his superiors for chopping off malefactors' ears in the old Indian style.

Few of the old cults had survived and south India was saturated with Brahminism. Some people professed themselves nauseated by Hinduism, the phallic symbol, the Shiva lingum, garlanded with flowers, the profusion of half-human, half-animal gods, with their multiple arms and legs, and found the atmosphere of a Hindu temple revolting. I felt none of this. The old cruelties had long disappeared. The family parties visiting a temple to worship were a cheerful sight, like Italian peasant families visiting their churches on feast days in their best clothes and in the true holiday spirit which is no longer seen at our formal, cold church festivals in the north.

The Tamil country bred holy men, genuine and fraudulent. In Pondicherry an ashram, a kind of Hindu monastery, had been founded by Arabindo Ghosh, the famous political rebel who had fled from British India in the days when imprisonment was not the prelude to public office. He acquired a profitable reputation

for saintliness and the power of healing, with the help
of an efficient middle-aged Frenchwoman, who became
known throughout south India as 'the mother'. Flocks
of pilgrims came from all over India to consult her
and on rare occasions, once or twice a year, to have the
dharshan of Sri Arabindo, that is, to see Mr Ghosh.
A member of a distinguished family, who had taken
one of the sons to Pondicherry for a consultation on
alcoholism, told me that 'the mother' confined herself
to giving practical advice. She asked what the doctor
had recommended and often merely endorsed his
opinion. The treatment was presumably a form of faith
healing, which gave the patient the mental strength
to persist in the necessary physical treatment.

An ingenious practitioner of a baser order stationed
himself in a ravine with a clear echo. Women would
come to ask him whether they would have children. He
shouted the question into the ravine, phrasing it so as to
end with the interrogative form of the verb 'to be',
'irrukalama?' Echo obligingly answered, 'Am A', meaning 'Yes'. It was a neat form of confidence trick and
doubtless profitable to the oracle. But the holy men
were by no means all crooks. Following the Hindu
tradition, there were many mystics, widely revered
throughout the south.

The most southerly district of the Madras Presidency, Tinnivelly, where I spent the last two months
of my time in the Madras civil service, had been a
favourable field for the missionaries, since it was full
of the depressed classes who were oppressed by the caste
Hindus, and to whom therefore Christianity offered
a new hope in life. In those days, before the establishment of the United Church of South India, sects pro-
liferated. In one village there were nine, including the
British missionary bodies, S.P.G. and C.M.S., roughly
high and low, which were treated as different sects,
and a local invention known as Hindu Christians, who
presumably tried to make the best of both worlds.

In another tiny village was a vast church with holes in the roof and only a handful of congregation. It had been built during a famine when the people, despairing of their own gods, were converted en masse to Christianity. It was said that the next year, after a good harvest, the converts relapsed to the faith of their forefathers, which, if the story was true, suggests a failure of logic.

Catholics and Protestants were often in opposition. I have tried a village riot case with the Indian Catholic priest supporting one side and the Indian Protestant priest the other. One of them was lying. It was widely believed, presumably by the Protestants, that the Catholic priests sometimes paid for one side's witnesses, either to protect their flock or under promise of conversion. Whatever the truth of these stories, I acquired in those few months a sincere admiration for the European Catholic missionaries. They lived as villagers on a tiny salary, they never went to the hills and they took home leave either every ten years or not at all. I realised that it can be harder to live than to die for your faith. They sensibly went much further than the Protestants in assimilating the ceremonies of the church to the local scene. Their churches were often hardly distinguishable from the Hindu temples, and the processions in honour of a favourite saint, such as St Anthony or the Virgin, might have been Hindu processions in honour of Vishnu or Mariyamma. One of the best of the Protestant missionaries was Howard Somervell, the Everest climber, who spent the whole of his working career as a doctor without salary or fees, in a missionary settlement containing lepers, in the days when leprosy was still incurable. Every day he made a point of touching some of them as he passed, so that they should not have the terrible feeling that they were excluded from all human contact except that of their fellow-sufferers.

Missionaries and Government officials did not always

see things in the same way. A notorious robber chief, Jambalingam Nadar, was converted in prison by a forceful lady missionary, Miss Amy Carmichael. The story current in non-missionary circles was that she had read him the account of St Paul's escape from prison, with the result that the next day he was out. The police asserted that after his escape he was as much of a robber as ever. According to their account, they laid a trap for him in a village where he was visiting his girl friend, surrounded the house and shot him in the course of a gun battle. They alleged that Miss Carmichael's two lady assistants, who lived in the village, gave statements at the time supporting the police version of the affair, but changed their story as soon as Miss Carmichael appeared on the scene. Miss Carmichael published her version, accusing the police of setting fire to the house where Jambalingam innocently lay and thus brutally murdering a man who had trod the path of virtue since his conversion. The English superintendent of police was equally emphatic in support of his version and I did not regard him as a liar. Both sincerely believed their version of the incident. It was an interesting example of the fallibility of historical evidence. I have no idea what the truth was.

South Indian education had benefited greatly from missionary endeavour, and generations of Indians had cause to be grateful to the Madras Christian College. For some worthy men of God the political situation provided a painful dilemma. They were anxious to avoid the charge that they were part of the foreign 'establishment', which was apt to give them a bias in favour of the political movement against the Government. Some adopted the Indian dress and way of life and tried to become as Indian as possible, though I doubt if it helped their cause. Some actively supported the independence movement. Their dilemma was that their sympathy for all things Hindu, their effort to understand the best in the Hindu religion, made it difficult for them to maintain the position that salvation could come only through Christianity, the true revealed religion, and that all other religious beliefs were false. It was more consistent with their outlook to hold the view, reached by George Trevelyan in his Indian letters, that all religions were different ways to God. In one instance at least, a sincere Christian missionary deserted his faith and found refuge in anthropology and a bride from the tribes which he was studying.

Between Tinnivelly and the ugly little port of Tuticorin which was my headquarters, there was a strange little community who lived in a small circular fort with mud walls about ten feet high. They remained strictly endogamous, although there were only a few hundred left. The men came out to till the fields; the women never came out for the whole of their lives. No policeman or Government official ever went inside, nor did any villager so much as look over the wall. The force of social custom in south India was strong. Here my brief period of service in British India ended and I moved to the Indian States.

5

THE INDIAN POLITICAL
SERVICE

THE Indian Political Service, which I joined on
leaving Madras, was recruited from the Indian army
and the Indian Civil Service, two soldiers to one civilian, because the finance department had told Curzon it
would be cheaper that way. In its final form, the service
consisted of two branches, the Political Department
with the Viceroy as its head and the External Affairs
Department under the Government of India. The
Political Department conducted political relations with
the Indian States which were not British territory,
through political residents and political agents under
them, acting as representatives of the Paramount
Power. The External Affairs Department administered
the North-West Frontier Province, which Curzon had
separated from the Punjab, the political agencies in
the frontier States, Baluchistan, the consulates in Central Asia, East Persia and the Gulf, and relations with
Afghanistan, Tibet and Nepal. The Government of
India's relations with other countries were conducted
through the British Foreign Office, but an embryo
diplomatic mission was established in Washington during the war and India was separately represented in

the League of Nations and at the Paris peace conference in 1946.

There had been old rivalry between the Foreign Office and the Government of India over relations with Persia, as it was then called, the highlight of the comedy being the despatch of Sir John Malcolm in 1807 by the Government of India, with the object of thwarting the designs of Napoleon, simultaneously with the despatch of Sir Harford Jones by the British Government. The demarcation dispute had been settled by the Foreign Office taking the Embassy at Teheran and the consulates in the north, while the Government of India took the consulates in the south and east where Indian interests were most concerned. In Central Asia there was an amicable division between the Indian 'politicals' who took Kashgar, and the China consular service which took Urumchi.

The Political Service had an exciting, romantic range of posts. Life in it was more glamorous than life in British India and it therefore attracted some jealousy from the other services. The 'civilians' in the Government of India and the provinces considered that the fabric of government depended on them, that the 'politicals' consisted of 'civilians' who shirked hard work and soldiers who did not get on in their regiments; and that they spent their time shooting and feasting with Maharajas and tribesmen. The generals who took the hospitality of the princes were only too inclined to believe that their pet princes, who had given them those wonderful tiger shoots, were unsympathetically treated by interfering political officers, a view sedulously inculcated by their hosts. Some soldiers on the frontier felt that they could manage things much better than the 'politicals' who were far too identified with the Pathans, being unable to understand that, with the sanctuary of Afghanistan behind, conditions for a satisfactory war did not exist and that the customary mixture of carrot and stick was the best way of keeping the frontier quiet without getting too deeply involved. It is strange to look back only thirty years to the days when the Maharajas had power in their States and believed that it would last for ever, when the Political Service had a mission in Llasa and a consulate in Chinese Turkestan, and when Colonel Schomberg was wandering round the Altai mountains with his two faithful Sherpas, promising to make you very comfortable for the night, if you happened to be in those parts. The Maharajas are now a dispossessed relic, while Chinese Turkestan and Tibet are, sadly, out of bounds.

Until 1944 I was almost wholly concerned with the Indian States. There were several hundred States, ranging from Hyderabad, with an area of 83,000 square miles and a population of fourteen and a half million, to tiny village States of a few square miles. Britain was the protecting power by virtue of a network of treaties and engagements. The Rulers were responsible for the internal administration of their States, but Britain, as paramount power, reserved the right to depose a Ruler for gross maladministration. In the largest States there was little need for interference in their internal affairs, though by no means all the Rulers of the largest States had been immune from British intervention. In the smaller States the political officer was often required to intervene. When the Ruler was a minor or had been deposed, the political officer took over the administration until the new Ruler was old enough to be put in charge.

The principal Residents in the Indian States lived in a grand way in order to keep up with the princes. They were appointed personally by the Viceroy. In Curzon's time the Residency at Hyderabad fell vacant and was coveted by Sir David Barr, a senior and bald member of the service. He telegraphed to Curzon, who was then in Simla: 'Psalm 132, verse 1', which, being interpreted, read, 'Lord, remember David'. Curzon replied with 'Psalm 75, verse 6': 'For promotion cometh neither from the East, nor from the West, nor from the South.' Barr was presumably encouraged, since Curzon was in the north. He telegraphed: 'Psalm 121, verse 1', 'I will lift up my eyes to the hills from whence cometh my help.' Curzon rounded off the series neatly with 'II Kings, 2, verse 23', 'Go up, thou bald head.'

The Indian princes loved titles, honours and ceremonial. The old Maharaja of Patiala collected decorations from foreign courts like stamps and had them specially reproduced in three-quarter size to get them all on his chest, which made him look like an old-fashioned swimming instructor when he had them all on. Precedence was regulated by gun-salutes, twenty-one downwards, the prefix of 'His Highness' being given to those with eleven or more. There had been periods of inflation, especially after the first war, as a result of which quite unimportant Rulers had grand titles and a liberal allowance of guns. The Resident visiting a State had to see that he got his gun-salute, in order to maintain the prestige of the representative of the King Emperor. The Resident for the Punjab States visited Patiala at a time when he was having a dispute with the Maharaja. He was given his salute, but the Maharaja put half charges in the saluting guns, so that the boum-boum became peep-peep, neatly indicating the Maharaja's displeasure.

Rajas with less than eleven guns often tried to call themselves 'His Highness the Maharaja of ...' and were sat on. No Ruler was allowed to call his son 'Prince', since that would suggest that he was himself a king. The Rulers had their own orders, titles and decorations in their States, but were not allowed to imitate the British version too closely. The formal title of the Maharaja of Gwalior was 'His Highness Maharaja Mukhtar-ul-Mulk, Azim-ul-Iqtidar, Rafi-ush-shan, Wala Shikoh, Mohta-sham-i-Dauran, Umdat-ul-

Umara, Maharadhiraja Alijah Hisam-us-Sultanat
George Jivaji Rao Scindia Bahadur, Shrinath Mansur-
i-Zaman, Fidwi-i-Hazrat-i-Malik-i-Muazzam-i-Rafi-ud-
Darjat-i-Inglistan, Maharaja of Gwalior.'

Precedence was of great importance. The famous
old Maharana of Udaipur found himself in a serious
dilemma when invited to King George V's Coronation
Durbar at Delhi. He was head of the most aristocratic
princely house, but only had nineteen guns. A few
upstarts of inferior descent had twenty-one guns and
he would have to sit below them. He could not do that,
nor could he show disrespect to His Majesty. He came
to Delhi with a great following. On the morning of
the Durbar he took enough poison to make himself ill
and prevent him from attending it. To have feigned
illness would have been dishonourable; the excuse had
to be genuine.

When the Chamber of Princes was meeting in Delhi,
the Viceroy held a grand dinner for the princes. Decid-
ing the precedence was difficult, since Rulers with the
same number of guns had precedence in their own
agency, but not outside it. Every year there were complaints. In 1935 the Viceroy invited King George of
Greece, on a visit to Delhi, and fifty princes, two, the
Rulers of Bikaner and Bundi, having been declared
to be equal in precedence and never to be invited to
the same party. It was a puzzle. We solved it happily
by asking King George to take fifth place and telling the
Maharao of Bundi, with some deviation from the truth,
that Her Excellency had specially asked that he should
sit next to her and that therefore the position of the
Maharaja of Bikaner next to His Excellency did not
mean that he was being put first.

The old ceremonial was rigidly observed, especially
when the Viceroy was visiting a State. It started with
a formal call and return call an hour later. The exact
point at which the host greeted the guest had to be
determined, usually one pace from the threshold. Both

visits were closed by the presentation of *itr* and *pan*, scent on the handkerchief and betel leaf, to those qualified to receive it, in order of precedence. The political officer had every kind of fancy dress for these occasions, even riding breeches with a gold stripe, though that was obsolescent in my time. A Ruler visiting the Chamber of Princes had the right to be met by an officer in uniform. Grumbling and in a bad temper, I pulled myself out of bed, clambered into 'undress', frock coat faced with braid, mameluke sword clanking on the ground, white pith helmet with gold spike and chain, tight trousers fastened under shiny boots, and drove myself down to the Delhi station in an ancient Dodge car, ready to meet the Maharaja of Benares as he stepped out of his special carriage precisely at 8.30 a.m. I threaded my way through the crowd of commuting clerks, pedlars, tea and *pan* sellers. No Maharaja. He had left. I have never felt so ridiculous. He had the grace to apologise. There was always the problem when to wear spurs. 'Don't you know, my dear fellow, that you don't wear spurs with levée dress?' said the fussy expert in Viceroy's House. 'Thank you very much,' replied the Irishman who had got it wrong. 'What a good thing that no one of any importance has noticed it.'

The political officer was not concerned only with these trivialities. History had bequeathed him a peculiar situation. The treaties with the States had been made at a time when the civil administration in British India amounted to not much more than the collection of revenue, the suppression of organised crime, and assistance to the army, when travelling 'up the country' was a dangerous undertaking without military protection, and when the treatment by a prince of his probably unfortunate subjects was of little interest in Calcutta or Leadenhall street. In later years, the Political Department, hampered by the old treaties, was attacked by critics from either wing, for bureaucratic interference with the Ruler's rights and for indolent complaisance in the face of oppression.

A political officer endowed with a modicum of imagination realised how infuriating it must be for a Ruler to have a busybody sitting on his doorstep, and viewed with amused tolerance the Ruler's efforts to distract his attention from a scrutiny of the State budget and inspection of the local prison by the offer of bread and circuses or, to be more precise, whisky and tigers. Perhaps, after all, the 'politicals' were the Maharajas' only real friends. Although they often wished the political officer to the devil, he was part of their system. He was their scourge or their governess, but also their prop. They tried to best him, but, in the final instance, they looked to him to protect them. At the same time, if the political officer had a conscience, he knew how often he was faced with oppression, but powerless to prevent it, and he knew then only too well what people were thinking when they saw him leave after a round of entertainment with no apparent consciousness of what was beneath the fair surface so carefully prepared for him.

A few States were as well administered as the neighbouring British provinces, but many were too small to provide a standard of administration in any way comparable with that in British India. A well-administered State was the most satisfactory form of local government evolved in India, since it was Indian, not alien, and was founded on the personal relationship between the Ruler and his people, which was deeply embedded in Indian tradition. A good Ruler was there for life. The collector in a British district (called deputy commissioner outside the old presidencies), however able and sincere, was likely to be moved every few years and remained a comparative stranger to the people of his district. There were many good men among the princes, who tried to administer their States decently, but in nearly all of them there was a lack of men and money to run them properly and, particularly in the smaller States, there were many abuses. Conditions in a State with a bad Ruler could be appalling.

The political officer struggled against the odds. When it became clear that a Ruler could not be left in charge of his State, he was entitled, if he was in the more important class, to ask for a commission of inquiry, in which other Rulers participated and he could have his case presented by a lawyer. The Ruler was therefore protected from arbitrary action by the Political Department. But the political officers did not act without good reason and it was rare for a Ruler in this position to accept a commission with all the ventilation of his follies or crimes which it involved. When a political officer took over a State after the deposition of a Ruler, the administration improved, the State treasury was replenished and in due course the State was handed over to a new Ruler who, only too often, had soon run it down to its previous condition. It was only a patching operation.

A perennial problem in almost all save the few large States which could manage their finances like a British province, was to determine what proportion of the State revenue it might be considered reasonable for the Ruler to spend on the upkeep of himself and his family. If the Ruler was taking too much, the political officer had the delicate and difficult task of pressing him to take less. A few years before independence, a committee of the Chamber of Princes and the Political Department tried to work out guide lines. We were discussing the Ruler's responsibility for the maintenance of his predecessor's family. The Maharaja of Patiala left the room for a moment. The Jam Sahib of Nawanagar, then President of the Chamber of Princes, laughed and said, 'This question is very important to him. He has fifty-five brothers and sisters.'

In the small States the officials were often hard put to it to maintain solvency. Their expedients were often ingenious. A political agent in Rajputana, visiting a small State, was surprised to see the chief minister sitting disconsolately by the side of the road, deep in thought. He asked what was the matter. The minister replied that the State elephant had eaten his budget appropriation and there were still three months to go. He would have to find ways and means. On his next visit, the political agent asked how the problem had been solved. The minister replied that they had reappropriated funds from the provision for food for the prisoners in the State gaol. The political agent asked, 'But will the prisoners not starve?' The minister finally produced the rabbit out of the hat: 'We found that last Thursday was the Duke of Connaught's birthday and, in honour of that great event, we released forty-seven prisoners.'

There were endless quarrels and intrigues in the little jungle capitals. The young Ruler, educated in one of the special schools established by the British and run on public school lines for the families of the Rulers and top families of the States, provided thereby with a slight knowledge of history, English literature and mathematics, a competent cricketer perhaps, entered his inheritance. He now probably lived in a tumble-down fort, surrounded by uneducated courtiers intent on indulging his whims and exploiting his vices, meeting with no criticism or restraining hand, occupying himself with a little administration, some tiger-shooting and the submissive society of the State officials in the local club, most of them villagers like himself. The lessons of the English school faded. Which of us would have resisted these surroundings? It was surprising that so many did. It was worse for the members of the Ruler's family, having no responsibility in the State, but so often not allowed to make a career outside, for fear of compromising the status of the family. It was not the men; it was the system that was at fault.

The political officer was involved in quarrels over

inheritance, since the Ruler's heir had to be recognised by the paramount power. One Ruler had quarrelled with his eldest son and worked hard to prove to the Political Department that he had only been married after the boy's birth and that therefore his favourite younger son was the rightful heir. Another, intent on disinheriting his elder son, claimed that he had been substituted for a girl at birth. In that case, we asked, why had he invited the Viceroy to his elder son's wedding?

A young Raja asked for my help. His sister had married another Raja who had turned her out of his house while she was pregnant, on the ground that he was not the father of the child. The young man wanted a reliable witness to be present at the birth to prove that a boy had not been substituted for a girl. A lady doctor from a neighbouring mission obliged. A girl was born. The young Raja commended his own honesty, since, he told me, his family had been urging him to substitute a boy, if a girl had been born.

We tried to compose the quarrels which disrupted life in these small self-contained societies, so isolated from the world outside. A childless Ruler had adopted an heir, quarrelled with him and managed to produce two sons, thus neatly turning the tables on the adopted son. This caused endless family quarrels after the father's death. The Ruler told me, 'When we were young, we were sitting down for our evening meal with our mother when, fortunately, someone sneezed. So we gave the food to the dog and the dog died.' In another State the adopted heir's natural parents used to frighten their son by telling him that the party opposing his succession were trying to poison him in milk. He could no longer swallow milk. It could have been true or it could have been only an attempt by the boy's parents to keep their hold on him in his new and powerful position. The quarrels between a Ruler's wives could cause great trouble and

were a convincing argument for monogamy. I urged
a Ruler to make his two wives compose their quarrels.
Some time later, he told us with satisfaction that he
had had them both in bed with him at the same time in
Bombay. With every new baby from the Ruler's wives
taking it in turn, the education budget was probably
cut a bit more. We could not help getting mixed up
in these family affairs.

The political officer's main concern in an agency
composed of small States was to see that the administration and finances were in reasonable order, without
unnecessarily interfering in the Ruler's internal
sovereignty, at least in theory. Except in the worst
cases, it was a matter for firm, but tactful persuasion.
The little Rulers' ideas of what constituted a legitimate
exercise of authority could be odd. A Muslim Ruler of
a tiny State in the middle of nowhere, who used to
auction the civil cases in his courts, complained bitterly,
when we interfered, that he would lose his judicial
income. I had to persuade an intelligent Maharaja,
whom I genuinely liked, to dismiss his finance minister
who had his hand in the till. The Ruler said frankly
that there was one difficulty. I would not believe it,
but he could assure me that the minister was the best
man in a hundred miles at raising spirits from the dead.
The Ruler was a reasonable man and we managed to
arrive at a suitable arrangement by which the minister
relinquished his official duties and continued his
spiritual private practice. It was an uphill task.

Stories of bribery were common, though I never
heard of a political officer being directly offered a bribe
to decide in someone's favour. Suggestions that bribes
had been taken by British officials usually originated in
the employment of agents who pretended to have
passed on the money, but had really kept it for themselves. The British Government recognised the Nawab
of Bhopal as heir to the old Begum against the Muslim
law of succession, after the old Begum had paid a special

visit to London to plead the case. It was widely believed in India that Lord Birkenhead must have accepted a large bribe, presumably on the calculation that there was no other conceivable reason for the British Government's decision. The people in India underrated the ability of the Government's lawyers to find learned arguments in law to enable the Government to do what they wanted, which was to do what the Begum wanted. After the deposition of the Maharaja of Bharatpur, an item was found in the accounts relating to a bribe allegedly given to the political secretary in Delhi. The bribe was, of course, never offered. Presumably the agent had kept the money, knowing that he could make the mad Maharaja believe anything.

After Sir Lepel Griffin, a most distinguished and honourable member of the Political Department, had left the post of Agent to the Governor-General in Indore (the old name for Resident in Central India), an Englishman asked someone in the neighbourhood whether he did not regard Sir Lepel Griffin as an outstandingly good man. The reply was no, on the ground that Sir Lepel had never decided matters the way he was paid. It was found that two men had made a handsome living out of a simple device. They had boasted that they were in touch with Sir Lepel Griffin and were in a position to get services performed for a bribe. When asked for evidence in support of their claim, they invited the prospective client to watch outside the gate of the Residency any Wednesday at 11 a.m., which they said was the fixed weekly time when they did their business there. All they had to do was to go through the front gate, hide in the shrubbery or visit the servants or the clerks. At an earlier date, the old Maharaja of Indore, who was in trouble, had presented the Agent to the Governor-General with one of those albums of photographs which are never opened. It was put on a shelf and no one looked at it until a visitor turned over the pages and found a note for a thousand rupees between the photographs. You could not be too careful.

The rules about accepting presents had not changed since the days of Charles Trevelyan's battle with Sir Edward Colebrooke. If you could not give the present back without giving offence, you had to put it in the *toshakhana*, the Government of India's treasure house, from which, if you wished, you could buy it back. Wedding presents valued at more than £15 had to be treated in the same way. My wife lost two dressing-cases through this rule, one of which, to her disgust, was afterwards presented by the Government of India to the Maharaja of Nepal. She received an emerald ring, given out of genuine friendship by a young and unsophisticated Maharani. She wore it for one evening and then we gave it back.

The political agent was living in Indian India, often in attractive country full of history and the remains of the past. He was living on natural terms with Indians who had no sense of inferiority nor major political grievances. He took part in their lives and stayed in their houses, and they stayed with him, with only the trifling disadvantage that their servants were accustomed to leave the lights and fans full on day and night. He was dealing with people, many of them sincere and friendly, the majority of whom were trying in the face of all the obstacles inherent in their situation, to fulfil according to their lights the obligations imposed on them by the accident of birth. It was an open-air life with plenty of free sport. The political agent had a fascinating job, but he knew that he was propping up a system which had outlived its time and which, for better or worse, would not survive.

6

CENTRAL INDIA

THE Agent to the Governor-General in Indore was furnished by a beneficent Government with a grand house with rows of columns and a classical portico, three political agents, two secretaries of which I was the junior, his own little kingdom stretching a mile or two round the house, complete with police, gaol, schools and hospitals, a copy of Aitchison's treaties, a flag, and a local Maharaja. Ten miles away was a general, and a lot of Gunners who occupied themselves in hunting jackal, sticking pig and shooting anything not reserved for a neighbouring Raja. It was an agreeable life.

Indore was ruled by the Maharaja Yeshwant Rao Holkar, descendant of one of the great Maratha chiefs who had had the misfortune to come up against the British just as they were about to grab most of the north Indian plain. The Maharaja's grandfather, Sivaji Rao, was slightly mad. He used to sit in a high window in the old city palace watching the passers-by. Anyone wearing a black coat was hauled up the stairs and was lucky if he escaped with only the coat taken away from him. Sivaji Rao came to grief and was deposed. His son, Tukoji Rao, also came to grief through bad luck. His girl of the moment had run away to a rich Parsee in Bombay and his men went to Bombay to get her back. There was a fight in the Bombay streets in which the Parsee was killed. A six foot six British Sapper officer happened to come along and intervened. The men fled. The Maharaja was offered a commission of inquiry, but chose to abdicate. He was an amiable weak man with three wives, two Indian and one American, known as the first, second and third mothers, each being entitled to a segment of the national anthem. At garden parties the guests, like fish in a temple tank rising to bread crumbs, were continually having to stand up for the arrival of a new mother, identified by the length of anthem allotted to her.

No Maharaja of Indore would live in his father's palace. Tukoji Rao built himself a palace in the Waring and Gillow style. The Maharaja of our day, Yeshwant Rao, had a modern palace designed by the German son-in-law of his Belgian private secretary, whose pleasant family lived permanently free on the Maharaja. Yeshwant Rao, tall, slender, with a curving frame, looked as if he would break in two in a strong wind. He too had his troubles and an American wife or two and died young. They were not a lucky family.

Indore was a centre of Jain merchants, who by their faith must try to avoid hurting any living thing. Jain devotees wear a pad over their mouths to make sure that they do not swallow an insect. Every twelve years a famous Jain festival was celebrated in the old city of Ujjain, not far from Indore. A long string of Jain holy men went in procession through Indore on their way to this festival, all nearly, some completely, naked, riding on elephants and bicycles, in carts or on foot, preceded by the State band playing the 'British Grenadiers'. The richest Jain merchant lived in an excessively ugly mansion with a garden full of monumental mason's statues, separated by a wall from the main road. Wishing to revive his failing sexual powers, he summoned Dr Voronoff to apply his monkey gland treatment. It was immediately spread about that the monkeys had died, as they presumably had. The uproar among the Jain community was formidable. So the old millionaire captured two monkeys and exhibited them in a cage on the wall to show that no monkeys had been killed. The device was apparently effective.

The Central India Agency contained all kinds of States, spread over several hundred miles and interspersed with bits of British India. After Indore, the most important State was Bhopal, now the capital of the State of Madhya Pradesh in the Indian Federation. It contained the famous Buddhist stupa of Sanchi and was ruled by the notable Hamidullah Khan, a favourite of the British, completely fearless, a brilliant polo player and shot, who killed his tigers on foot and whose redoubtable daughters used to indulge in the equally dangerous sport of hockey on roller-skates on the marble floor of one of the family's palaces. Nawab Hamidullah Khan was a notable figure in princely politics. He was not an easy man for the political agent to handle, since he made full use of his influence in London and Delhi to squash any action of the political officer which he disliked. He later tried but failed to keep his State out of the Indian Federation.

Another notable character in a smaller way, in the Malwa Agency, was the Nawab of Jaora, whose ancestor had been a successful bandit at the time of Sir John Malcolm's settlement of Central India. The British officer who confirmed him in his State had the brilliant idea of diverting him from hunting men by introducing a pack of hounds, which was hunted for three generations up to the 1930s.

In 1933 the A.G.G., as he was universally called, was Lieutenant Colonel Rawdon Macnabb, a man of principle and integrity for whom I had both affection and admiration. He had an attractive and friendly approach and there was no hint of superiority in his manner. The senior secretary, Billy Egerton, who was responsible for the political work, had won all the classical prizes at Eton and Trinity. With a splendidly

unconventional wife, who cared nothing for the shib-
boleths of Anglo-India, he bore no resemblance to the
stuffier type of official. Fifteen miles from Indore was
the village of Dewas, divided by the main road. As a
result of historical accident arising out of a quarrel
between two brothers a hundred years before, the State
of Dewas had been divided into two. On the one side
of the road the Ruler was the Maharaja of Dewas
Senior, on the other the Maharaja of Dewas Junior,
each Maharaja being entitled to the title of 'His Highness' and a salute of fifteen guns. It was a comic
absurdity.

In 1921 E. M. Forster had been secretary to the
Maharaja of Dewas Senior, of whom he has written in
The Hill of Devi, including the last episode of the
Maharaja's career in 1933, long after Forster had left
the State. The Maharaja, whom Forster described as
'certainly a genius and possibly a saint', was clearly a
man of considerable charm. Sir Malcolm Darling, an
outstanding member of the Punjab civil service, who
had been his guardian, was devoted to him and never
failed to support him to the inglorious end of the
story.

The facts of the case which Forster relates are clear
enough. The Maharaja's son, later Maharaja of Kol-
hapur, ran away from the State, believing that his father
was trying to poison him. The Maharaja spent large
sums on family ceremonies and secret agents and, with
the help of a slump in agricultural prices, the State
went bankrupt. The State officials were not paid their
salaries and many of the unfortunate cultivators, who
were heavily over-taxed, were forced to sell their land.
Finally, the Government had to intervene. They
rejected the Maharaja's request for a large loan and
offered him the alternative of either agreeing to accept
an accounts officer to prepare a financial report, or
appointing a new chief minister nominated by the
Government of India, undertaking not to dismiss him.

The Maharaja prevaricated and failed to answer within the stipulated time. The Government therefore offered him a commission of inquiry. The Maharaja pretended to go on a pilgrimage to south India and, when he was there, ran away to Pondicherry, the capital of French India, where the Government of India could not get at him, taking with him all the valuables of the State on which he could lay his hands, even including the silver trappings of the elephant howdahs. He refused to return and died in Pondicherry.

Forster suggests that the political officers were wrong in rejecting the Maharaja's 'friendly approach', and quotes him as saying that the Government of India's orders 'dishonoured him in the eyes of his subjects and his fellow chiefs'. Basing himself presumably on memories of earlier days, Forster writes:

> Unfortunately most of the A.G.G.s and P.A.s he had to deal with were not the sort of people whom he wanted as friends and negotiators; nor can I feel surprised; I have experienced them myself. They were insensitive, or, if they were sensitive, they were clever-clever and tried to beat him at his own tricks, and one or two of them were cads. There were exceptions, but on the whole they constituted an unattractive body of men.

Of the Maharaja's time in Pondicherry, Forster writes that his friends advised him to give in to the inevitable. 'He ignored our advice, and naturally, for royal blood ran in his veins and not in ours. He was descended from the sun.' In cold fact, he had no royal blood in his veins, being descended from a mere officer of the Peshwa, the hereditary prime minister of the old Maratha State.

I fear that Forster's judgement was clouded by his old affections, mixed, it seems, with a tinge of mockery. How could Rawdon Macnabb have recommended a loan? The Maharaja had ruined his little State through improvidence and selfishness. He had quarrelled with his son, who was a man of ability and character. He could not be left in unfettered control of the destinies of his unfortunate subjects, whom he had left destitute. The conditions offered had been reasonable, not harsh. I remember the last visit paid by the Maharaja to Macnabb. He was received with a courtesy and friendship which he did not merit. He must by that time have already decided to run away and take everything he could with him. In a case like this, typical of many, the political officer could not win.

In Forster's account the Maharaja 'would point out indignantly that other Rulers – Alwar for instance – had behaved far worse, but had got off scot free because they were powerful, and that he himself – unlike others – had never wavered in his loyalty to the Crown'. Disloyalty to the Crown was not a profitable aberration for an Indian Ruler. His existence depended on the Crown and he had nowhere else to go. The Crown's enemies were the Maharajas' enemies. The Maharaja of Alwar did not get off scot free in the end. He was highly intelligent and affected great sanctity. His alleged crimes were numerous and picturesque. He called himself by the impressive title of the Raj Rishi, the Royal Teacher, and would not touch leather for fear of defilement. His fellow princes were not impressed. He arrived at Bharatpur, a neighbouring State, for a family wedding, to be met by a Rolls-Royce upholstered inside and out in leather, with chauffeur and footman dressed in leather from head to foot. Nor was the Crown impressed. At Buckingham Palace an equerry brought him a message that His Majesty would not shake hands with him unless he removed his gloves.

Finally, the Maharaja of Alwar overstepped the mark. A few days after a Resident, not known for his perspicacity, had described him as his brother in a

sentimental speech at a State banquet, his outraged
subjects rose against him, a very rare occurrence in the
States of those days. He was exiled and the administration of the State was taken over by the Political Department. He wrote to Sir Bertrand Glancy, then head
of the Political Department, to ask for the address of
an English friend. From Bombay, his place of exile,
he had been fomenting intrigues in his old State. Before
Glancy had replied to his letter, the Government of
India announced that he would not be allowed to
return to his State for fifteen years, which meant for
life, since by that time he was reputed to be living on
a mixture of port and brandy. Glancy answered his
letter, giving the address which he wanted. The Maharaja thanked him in a cordial reply, adding: 'P.S.
Thanks also for the fifteen years.'

7

LIGHT INTERLUDE IN
DELHI AND SIMLA

T H E scene shifts to imperial Delhi where the Vice-
roy sat enthroned in splendour in his grand palace.
In 1886, when the Viceroy still lived in Calcutta and
New Delhi was only a dream of the future, George
Aberigh Mackay, in his satirical account of the Indian
journey of Sir Ali Baba, described the Viceroy, the
Great Principal as he called him, in terms not so far
from Nehru's views at the end of British rule:

I never tire of looking at a Viceroy. He is the centre
of a world with which he has no affinity. He is a
veiled prophet. He who is the axis of India, the
centre round which the Empire rotates, is necessarily
screened from all knowledge of India. He lisps no
syllable of any Indian tongue; no race or caste, or
mode of Indian life is known to him; all our delight-
ful provinces of the sun that lie off the railway are
to him an undiscovered country; Moslems and
Hindus blend together in one dark, indistinguishable
mass before his eye. A Nawab often used to ask me
what the use of a Viceroy was. I do not believe that
he meant to be profane. I always replied with the
counter-question: 'What is the use of India?' He

never would see – the Oriental mind does not see these things – that the chief end and object of India was the Viceroy, that, in fact, India was the plant and the Viceroy the flower.

The picture was, of course, intentionally overdrawn and Mackay did not mean it to be taken too seriously, but there was some truth in it. However earnest and sincere, however well versed in Indian affairs the Viceroys were, they suffered from their splendid isolation and sometimes seemed to us lesser mortals to be even more insulated than the rest of us from the Indian life around them. But we recognised that no man in that position could escape from the shackles of the pomp and circumstance that went with that awesome position.

The great ceremonial of the Delhi winter season was the investiture, much grander and more formal than investitures in Buckingham Palace. Lutyens's grand Durbar hall was lined with members of the Viceroy's bodyguard, huge men in turbans, scarlet frock-coats and high boots, carrying lances with pennons. All the male guests wore uniform, cavalrymen looking more like Hollywood representations of Bengal Lancers than the real thing, the civilians in white knee breeches, silk stockings and buckled shoes. While the Viceroy's orchestra played 'God save the King', the procession entered, headed by the Viceroy in the superb light blue robes of the Star of India and the Vicereine in all the jewels which she had inherited or bought or borrowed for the job, their long trains held by the sons of Indian princes, whose necks were loaded with discoloured pearls from the State treasuries. Maharajas wore brightly coloured turbans and long brocaded tunics, with perhaps a diamond necklace to finish it off. It was the British version of the old Indian ways. They had built this splendid palace in the old capital. Here was the Mogul court in full array. It was in the historical

tradition of India and it pleased the British too with
their perennial passion for dressing up.

I was the humble under secretary in the Foreign
and Political Department, the most junior member of
the Political Service in it. I was responsible for procuring the insignia from England and handing them to the
Viceroy on a cushion. The date drew near and there
were no signs of the insignia of the Order of the Bath,
one G.C.B., two K.C.B.s and five C.B.s. I thought I
had located them in the middle of the Indian ocean.
The case was rushed off the ship and brought by air
to Delhi. I tackled it with a crowbar. Out tumbled a
cascade of medals of the Order of St John of Jerusalem.
There was no help for it. I had to borrow them. Lord
Chetwode had to lend his G.C.B. for presentation to
his bitterest professional enemy among the Delhi
generals. He grumbled: 'What am I to wear? Some
bloody Japanese decoration?', but was firmly reminded
that he had plenty more in the bag. We told Lord
Willingdon just before the Durbar began. He laughed.
Only the general who received the second-hand G.C.B.
murmured about what the palace would think, and his
liver was notorious. I breathed again.

There was more ceremony. A formal deputation in
full uniform waited on the Maharaja-Prime Minister
of Nepal to escort him to Viceroy's house. We moved
solemnly and silently down the steps of the Hyderabad
palace, lent for the occasion, each with his hand held
by a Nepalese in plumed helmet ornamented with
uncut emeralds. Suddenly it was like an ant-heap
stirred by a stick. People rushed in opposite directions.
The military secretary dropped his revolver. It was not
a bomb; we were too well protected for that. The
carriage was not there. The comic Muse had taken over.

I saw the edge of the foreign side too. The 'faqir of
Ipi' was causing trouble on the frontier. The new
consul in Kashgar in Central Asia had been told not to
take his wife. When he was well beyond Gilgit and out

of reach, he told us by wireless that she was with him.
No sympathy was subsequently expressed when she was
shot in the arm during the siege of the consulate. We
surprisingly found men to go to the Red Sea islands,
Perim at the foot and Camaran some hundreds of miles
up and I first heard the old story of the man who was
always asking to have his time extended in Perim, which
no one could understand until his commanding officer
met him walking down Piccadilly. I was to visit Perim
in 1967 just before the British finally left Aden, when
Members of Parliament with a fervid imagination pic-
tured it as being used to block the passage through
the Red Sea and I was recommending that we should
abandon Camaran in the hope that, like the snark, it
would softly and silently vanish away. In 1935 no one
dreamt that we were so near the end of empire.

In the spring, when the Horse Show was over and
the hot winds began to blow, the whole Government
moved to the hills and perched itself on the Simla
ridge. We took our horses with us and rode to office
past the General Headquarters where, as tradition had
it, the device of pyramidal self-promotion had been
invented, which enabled a captain to promote himself
successively to the rank of brigadier by increasing his
staff at suitable intervals, making it necessary for him
to be continually promoted in order to keep the establishment's pyramid in its proper shape. In this building an irate Commander-in-Chief, faced with a
'civilian's' memorandum full of Latin tags, had written
testily in red ink, 'All I can say is that this is nullum
sanguineum bonum'.

Nearby was the civil secretariat, where an ingenious
member of the Indian Civil Service had invented an
agricultural disease and happily watched the file grow
to vast proportions, without any expert being prepared
to admit that he had never heard of it. At the bottom
of the hill was the Viceregal Lodge, an accurate copy
of a Harrogate hydro, in which Lord Minto had once

presided over a debate between the proponents of differing systems of irrigation. He had fallen asleep. Waking suddenly at the moment when he was required to give his decision, he had remarked, 'No, my dear, I think we won't take the little dog for a walk.'

We rode out to dinner too. I soon acquired a distaste for being pulled up steep hills by the rickshaw coolies and used them as little as possible. In the past, there had been a few incidents of British callousness and stupidity. An Englishman had kicked a rickshaw coolie with an enlarged spleen. The coolie had died and the man was given eighteen months in prison. The next year, a rickshaw got out of control and the British occupant was hurled over the side of the hill. The coolies ran away to their homes and only reappeared cautiously in the next season. They were asked why they had run away, since the passenger had been unhurt. They replied with some sense that they had not waited to see. 'If a sahib was given eighteen months for killing a coolie, what wouldn't a coolie get for killing a sahib?' But we heard little of that sort of conduct which had caused so much bad blood in Curzon's day, and, when a shooting party from a British regiment got into trouble for beating up villagers, opinion was solidly against them. Manners had changed and the pressures of Indian nationalism were making themselves felt.

Simla life was not so very different from what it had been in Kipling's day – cars only for the Viceroy and the Commander-in-Chief, the shouts of the rickshaw coolies racing each other, the sedate pace of the Viceregal coolies in their smart liveries, six men pushing the fattest members of council up the steepest hill, the young men in perfectly cut jodhpurs taking their girl friends for a ride, known colloquially as doe-hacking, the riding parties to the Sipi fair where the marriageable girls were displayed to the prospective bridegrooms, the polo, horse shows and trotting races at Annandale, the new generation of Mrs Hawksbees, the social life centring on Viceregal Lodge, the appalling living conditions in the bazaar slum only a few feet below the elegance of the Mall. The best of all that happy, careless life was the day-long walks, down from 8,000 feet to 4,000 feet, up to 11,000 feet and back again, on the steep slopes of the Himalayan foot-hills, the hills crowned with little wooden temples, with glimpses of the ranges beyond and the feeling that Tibet was just round the corner.

It was a little self-centred society, with its own in-bred gossip – P. J. Grigg, the finance member of council, teasing Lady Willingdon by wearing a soft collar and a flower in his button-hole at Viceregal Lodge, knowing that she disapproved violently of both; the latest stage in his tempestuous relationship with Malcolm Muggeridge of the *Statesman*; the ever so gentlemanly courtship of the newest A.D.C. There were few scandals. The society was the reverse of permissive. It was still essentially a Victorian way of life, which has now gone for ever.

These trivial stories are part of the Simla saga and give something of the country-house atmosphere of the summers in Simla, so different in spirit from the more formal, less intimate life in those sprawling, impersonal bungalows hiding in their gardens in New Delhi. The migration was much criticised by the Indian politicians who were bred in the furnace heat of the plains. It died when the war came near India and numbers, efficiency and propriety inhibited the move. But while the Government of India was still small in numbers, in times of peace, there was much to be said for allowing the men who governed the country to deal with the problems of politics and administration in a climate in which they felt alive and vigorous, rather than in the heat of Delhi which, before the age of air-conditioning, exhausted body and mind.

8

GWALIOR

I T was not easy for a retired general who had been Resident in Hyderabad to bear with all the suspicions and intrigues which surrounded the young Maharaja of Gwalior. After a year the general was convinced that he was being spied on, which was probable, poisoned, which was improbable and the target of black magic, which was possible, though not necessarily effective. A year before, an attempt had been made to stop a marriage in an important family of the State by anonymous letters addressed to the bride's mother, threatening harm to the bride through magic. The mother stood firm and the girl was married. The letters went on, declaring, 'Now you have done it; you will see.' Four weeks passed, I hope of happiness for the bride. The couple were driving. The car went out of control and hit a tree. The husband was unhurt; the wife died of her injuries. Another letter came : 'I told you so.' It was cruel.

The general gave up and I became the Maharaja's guardian. I was not there to teach; there was an English tutor. There was a political and human requirement. The young man, aged seventeen, was to be invested with his ruling powers in a year's time. At the moment he was uncooperative through the influence of his mother and her relations. It would be difficult to give him the responsibility of ruling this great State if he remained in that frame of mind. But if he were not given his ruling powers, there would be endless trouble ahead. I was to try and bring him round. All I did was to become his friend. The rest followed as a matter of course.

The Maharaja's father had been a man of immense energy and dominating personality, with a wild side to him. A devoted friend of King George V and Queen Mary, he had named his children after them. He had enjoyed teasing his ministers. He started a hopeless task, to create a summer capital out of a village in the jungle almost as hot as Gwalior. He used to take his unfortunate ministers to work there with him for the whole day as labourers on road-making. On a tiger shoot the ministers were sometimes told to act as beaters. No tiger appeared for King Alfonso; the Maharaja was furious. The weary ministers arrived exhausted from the beat to see the motor-launch disappearing across the lake and face a long walk home. He dressed up as a cart driver to see if he could get past the guards into his own palace. His first wife, with a strong character like his own, remained in favour, even though she could have no children and her successor had a son, a most unusual situation in an Indian household. It was hard on the second wife, but her moment was coming. The Maharaja wore himself out and died. His first wife prudently died too.

The young Maharaja's mother was now firmly in control as President of the minority council formed by the Resident. She was behind the purdah and had little education and no experience of the outside world. It is difficult to talk to a curtain. Her son was her life. She wanted to guard him from his father's extravagances and to keep her own power. When I arrived, he had only her thoughts and suspicions. I was sorry for him. He had no real friends. He lived with his mother and her brother in the vast palace, where I could reach him only by prior arrangement. I lived in a large, gloomy mansion, with peacocks for decoration and peacocks squawking in the garden, outside the palace walls. I had to fight against a feeling of impotence, almost of suffocation. Could I ever win on those terms?

The members of the minority council were too pleased with themselves and it was not surprising that the Maharaja thoroughly disliked most of them. The Muslim member, a professional loyalist for his own purposes, had abused his position by inviting British generals to shoot the Maharaja's tigers, and suffered unattractively from swollen stomach, halitosis and swollen head. I had more respect for Sir Kailas Haksar, who used to give me Château Yquem in the morning in a temperature of 110°. The Maharaja loved the spring festival of Holi, as he could then squirt coloured water, mixed with oil to make it stick, on Sir Kailas, who had just come back from entertaining prime ministers at a commonwealth conference in London and found it hardly in keeping with his international position to have to sit in a bath for hours trying to get the paint off.

The atmosphere of Gwalior was insistent, almost overpowering. The picture remains vivid in the memory: the great fort overshadowing the town, the goldsmiths' street with the elaborately carved stone window screens, the huge State elephant swaying in the processions under the weight of the ceremonial howdah, the treasury with its coils upon coils of dead, discoloured pearls, the State guest house with its forms inviting guests to note their requirements – a car, a carriage or an elephant – the smell of dried cow-dung fuel, the screeching of the peacocks, the pervasive presence of white-skirted, scarlet-hatted figures, waiting to fulfil every wish, eternally making the symbolic gesture of obeisance, the hand sweeping the ground and raised to the head, as if placing dust on it, the Durbars with the rows of nobles seated on the floor, legs tucked underneath, curved swords at the side, and among them one little, incongruous European figure with florid face and flowing moustaches, sitting cross-legged, in grey top hat, grey frock coat, white socks and no shoes. He was the private secretary, the last in the line of Neapolitan adventurers who had attached themselves to the house of Scindia in the days of its glory in the eighteenth century and whose descendants had remained ever since in the Rulers' service. Over it all loomed the presence of the palace, with its unhappiness, its intrigues, against which I had to fight to help the boy to find out how to live a natural, happy life and to dispel the fears and suspicions which held him. For the first time I felt that I was really in India.

The Government of India had arranged that I should take the Maharaja to Lyallpur in the Punjab to see the agricultural research and revenue settlement going on there. He was not going to learn much that way; it was the change of surroundings that was important. He had never been parted from his mother and bitterly resented being made to go. His mother fought against it, but without success. The minister of education, who was a saint, came with us. Unfortunately he was a weak saint, unable to stand up against the maternal clique. The Maharani's brother came too. He was not a saint, only a spy. Every evening the boy telephoned to his mother; every evening the saint and the spy reported every action and every word. Gradually there came a change. The young man began to cheer up and enjoy himself. He was on his own for the first time. The Indian officials at Lyallpur flattered him and treated him as someone of importance. It was a new experience for him. I took him to Lahore, where we had lunch with the Resident for the Punjab States. That was one of the days when the Sikhs and Muslims went for each other by the Badshahi mosque, which was on our route home. I could not risk getting a Hindu Maharaja mixed up in that. I went to prospect, leaving him in the house. On the way home, I asked him if he had been all right. He said, 'The Resident was very kind to me. He gave me books and magazines to read, but then went out and *shut the door*.' In his experience doors were only shut to lock people inside.

We went to Calcutta for Christmas. Mother came too. We travelled in a special train for a thousand miles or so from the palace siding at Gwalior. On the Calcutta station an ant-heap of palace servants waited for us with a tent-wall, which closed round the Maharani as she left her carriage and shielded her from profane male eyes, including mine. For a widow no longer in her first youth it was an odd custom. I saw her once, when the curtain in the train blew aside.

The Christmas of 1935 was one of the last great Calcutta festivals of the British Raj: racing, polo, the Viceroy in residence in Belvedere, Warren Hastings's old house, a grand fancy-dress ball in eighteenth-century court dress against the background of those elegant houses of the period, the Viceroy and the dynamic and ruthless Lady Willingdon tempting Providence as Louis XVI and Marie Antoinette, the portly Sir John Anderson in wig and flowered waistcoat, our host at dinner in his imposing Government House modelled on Kedleston, looking as if he had stepped out of the pages of William Hickey. My ward enjoyed the racing. I said, 'Don't go in for racing quite so deeply as your father.' Soon after I had left, he had over two hundred horses in training and was winning all the best races with *Finalist*.

We were soon off again, without mother, for a little administrative training in Bangalore in the south, taking our horses with us, exercising them in the morning with the young Maharaja of Baroda, who had brought a Rolls-Royce upholstered in tiger skin. This time the Maharaja was delighted to go and thoroughly enjoyed himself. The atmosphere had completely changed. Back in Gwalior, my memory is of heat, com-

ing at you in waves from the early morning, as we
started the day in a muck sweat from the boy's favourite
amusement of riding up and down steep hills full of
loose rocks, and galloping the horses home, sweating,
on the hard road, in spite of my protests, in the hope
that my horse would run away with me. In May we
were to spend a few weeks in Poona. The train arrived
at Gwalior in the middle of the day. The drill was to
set out with a wet towel round the head, keep the
windows of the car tight shut against the scorching
wind, get in the burning hot train with a large block
of ice, eighty pounds of it, in a container between the
seats, dip a towel in the ice water and tie it under the
fan, shut the windows and shutters, dip your own towel
in the ice water and tie it round your head again, lie
down and hope that you would still be alive at the
other end. At Poona the priests were in a happy position. By the side of the Maharaja's house was the shrine
of his famous ancestor, Madhava Rao Scindia, whose
shade was provided every day with fresh offerings of
food and clothes. I presumed that the priests were
allowed to appropriate anything that Madhava Rao did
not want.

Our journeys continued with a trip to Rajputana to
visit other princes in neighbouring States and see how
they managed things. In Kotah, Charles Trevelyan's
first independent post a hundred years before, the old
Maharao sat in the club every evening clicking his false
teeth and playing a card game called jabbar with the
State officers, the only important rules being that the
Maharao could look at his neighbour's cards and had
to win. In Dholpur, having admired the stuffed
pheasant shot in Windsor Great Park with His Majesty
and his four sons, we shared the Maharajrana's daily
ritual. The car drew up on a jungle road and the driver
hooted. Up trotted a herd of wild deer and were fed
by the Ruler's men. One hind was being treated for a
sore throat, although she had never been in captivity.

The Maharajrana was unable to adjust himself to independence. After a year of it, he sent a Christmas card to his friends showing the young Maharaja of Gwalior, him and me in a boat on the lake which he had made into a bird and animal sanctuary, with the legend, 'Gone are the happy and peaceful days, alas!'

We could not buy a horse unless it had been certified sound by the expert on lucky marks – a most lucrative profession, I used to think. We were in the hands of the astrologers. We could start no journey except on an auspicious day. If it was a really bad day, you could do nothing about it. If it was neutral, you could get over the difficulty with a little trouble. On the nearest lucky day before we were due to leave, the Maharaja dedicated a groundnut in the temple. On the day of our departure, I started in a separate car and waited for the Maharaja on the road outside the town. He went to the temple and picked up the groundnut, thereby transferring the qualities of the very good day to the indifferently qualified day on which we were actually leaving. While the weather was still unpleasantly hot, we visited Simla to fix the detailed programme of the investiture with the Viceroy. It was pleasantly cool and I wanted to stay there as long as possible. In eight days we finished our business. The ninth day was unlucky; no good. On the tenth day there was an eclipse; also no good. The eleventh day was a fast day; still no good. So I had three extra days in the cool of Simla. Every morning the Maharaja had on his desk his programme for the day, with lucky and unlucky hours marked. It was a tiresome complication to life.

Tigers were reserved for the Maharaja and his guests. The villagers dared not shoot them, however much damage the tigers did to their cattle and goats. In one village where there was an especially troublesome tiger, the villagers shot him and put the corpse on the railway line to be run over by a train. The Maharaja's

father had tried to acclimatise African lions in the
Gwalior jungles, but they found it difficult to get their
food in the strange surroundings until they found that
old women could not run very fast. A drinking pool
was drugged and they were destroyed, though one survived to be shot in my time.

We saw many tigers that summer. One day I was
sent out by myself to shoot one. I am not a good shot.
A minor palace *shikari* took me to a wooded coombe,
through a passage protected by stone walls eight feet
high and up into a stone tower. The *shikari*, who had
about as little skill or experience as I had, had been
given only three cartridges. He fired from behind so
close to my face that the wadding hit me. There was
a whole family of tigers in the beat. I shot at one escaping up the hill and missed. A magnificent tiger leapt
across the stone passage. Fortunately, I missed again;
otherwise, he would have fallen, wounded and angry,
into the passage. I killed only a half-grown male, which
I would not have shot at if I had realised that it was
not fully grown. Another day, I wounded a tiger in the
paw. Later, the Viceroy was shooting in the same place.
A tiger turned back and wounded a beater. I believed
it was the same tiger and that therefore I was responsible.
I was not proud of my shooting efforts in Gwalior.
They were dangerous to others and unfair on the tigers.
Later, I went through the routine more competently.

One day I suggested to the Maharaja that I should
go with the beaters. He was horrified. It would be
impossible. If I were killed, people would say that he
had arranged it. On 1 April, when the temperature
was approaching 110°, the Resident received a message
that a tiger shoot had been arranged for him. He drove
fifteen miles in the blistering heat at midday to find
nothing. He had forgotten the whole-hearted Indian
addiction to the April fool joke.

Many scornful stories were told of the way the princes
doped their tigers for distinguished guests, and of the

unsporting conditions of a shoot in an Indian State. My sympathies were with the princes. They could not afford to risk an accident and they found by experience that some distinguished guests would happily overlook it if dubious means were used to get them a tiger and were furious if they did not get one. In Gwalior, when someone more important than I was shooting tiger, they placed the head *shikari* in a position to kill the tiger if the guest missed. There was a picture in the palace of one Viceroy standing over eight tigers. That was just greed. His sporting exploits in Gwalior in the early days of the minority administration had not done him much credit in the State. Otherwise intelligent people can be remarkably obtuse when it comes to sport. A Maharaja related to me with great amusement how he had ordered his men on a duck-shoot to collect every dead duck in sight, whoever had shot them, and pile them behind the butt of the Commander-in-Chief, for whom the shoot had been arranged. The guest declared that it was the best duck-shoot he had ever had.

As we came towards the date proposed for the investiture, the Maharaja was a changed person and was eagerly looking forward to his future responsibilities, but his relations with his mother inevitably became strained. She had learned nothing during the year. She did her utmost to prevent her son being put in charge of the arrangements for the ceremony and was determined to the end to keep her hold. She threatened to throw herself off the palace roof, but we did not believe that. Poor lady, she was advised badly and was bound to lose. I blamed her relations who saw power and position slipping away from them.

The Viceroy arrived in great pomp in his special train with a large British staff and over a hundred servants. It was what was expected of him and the State did not grudge the expense, since it gave honour to their Ruler; but I was distressed when the Maharaja told me that the Viceroy's servants demanded money during his visits to a State and even when the Maharaja went to Delhi. No one dared refuse, since the servants could easily make trouble and blame it on the State. I told the military secretary later, but I doubt whether he could have stopped this old custom. On the banqueting table was the late Maharaja's famous electric train of silver wagons, which passed slowly round the table on its silver rails in front of the guests, who could take nuts, fruit and wine from it as it passed and stop the train by lifting a decanter off the last two cars.

The Viceroy had, of course, to shoot his tiger. I had talked it over with the Maharaja, who did his best to give him an honest tiger. Lord Linlithgow was a good sportsman and would far rather have had nothing than a doped tiger. But the State prestige was involved. After several days, when no tiger appeared, he got one which seemed to move sleepily. The Maharaja avoided the subject. I did not blame him.

As the Maharaja took over his ruling powers, Sir Kailas Haksar said to him, 'My boy, I served your father for forty years. I dandled you on my knee, when you were a baby', the implication being that Sir Kailas should run the State for him. Good advice, no doubt, but the result was that, ten days later, the elder statesman found himself compulsorily lent to the Maharaja of Bikaner. I was not surprised. I left as soon as the investiture was over. I had, I think, become a genuine friend of the Maharaja. He was not easy on others nor on himself and was impatient of advice. In his position it was not surprising. I believe that the State was at least as well administered under him as it had been under the minority council. He married an able and attractive wife who made a name for herself in Indian politics. At the time of independence he accommodated himself sensibly to the new order of things. He died young and I never saw him again. It has all changed now. Something that was rooted in the soil has gone, but the young Maharaja who now enters on a new kind of career for a member of his family, has had a far happier and easier start to life than his father had with all his wealth and position.

9
MYSORE

Before dawn the car stuck fast in the sand of a dry river-bed which stretched into the distance. I saw lights and heard the familiar wailing music. Needing bullocks to pull the car out, I walked towards the lights. The villagers were fire-walking, the young nervously dashing across the burning pit, the old walking slowly and disdainfully, some even dancing a few steps in the middle, showing off. Fire-walking has been built up into an Eastern mystery. I saw no miracle; it seemed just a combination of faith and hard soles. I hope their gods gave them something good for it.

The Mysore State, where I was to be secretary to the Resident, was a great State with a sound administration built by a succession of able Brahmin ministers on the foundations laid by an interlude of fifty years of British rule. The Maharaja, gentle, dignified and wrapped in his religion, had achieved the peace of the contemplative life. He was as near to a constitutional monarch as India has ever seen. His nephew, the adopted heir, had never left the surroundings of a Hindu court, but had acquired a deep knowledge of European music. It needs imagination and tenacity to assimilate an alien culture in an intellectual atmosphere so wholly separated from anything outside the Hindu arts and religion. The Prime Minister, Sir Mirza Ismail, treated the State like one of Jane Austen's country gentlemen with a passion for 'improvements' and, we used unkindly to say, provided the eyewash which concealed the soundness of the administration. His coloured fountains were greatly admired by the populace, but not by aesthetic snobs like me.

Mysore was all that the tourist expected from the Orient. There were the temples with jagged symmetrical outlines covered in sculpture, seeming not to be imposed ornament, but to be part of the structure, so that a sharp edge presenting a uniform vertical line might be formed at one level by a body twisted to one side, a hip pushed out lasciviously and an arm raised above the head, at another by one trunk serving an elephant on either side. There was the huge monolith of Sravana Belgola, carved from the top of the hill on which it stood, a naked Jain *guru* or teacher, standing so still that the tendrils of a creeper wind round each arm. There were the great falls of Gersoppa, the fortresses romantically perched on almost inaccessible rocks, and the deserted city of Viyayanagar near the State border, abandoned after a final defeat by the Muslim kingdoms of the Deccan, with its stone streets, palaces and houses invaded by the roots of the banyan trees, the frieze on the throne platform showing the defeat of the kingdoms which were yet to take their revenge. The jungles were full of elephant, bison, tiger and panther. The ceremonial at the festival of *Dassera* was the finest in India; bejewelled prince immobile in his golden *howdah* on the largest, languorously swaying elephant in the Indies, the procession of elephant and camel carriages and, the climax of it all, the Durbar before the palace outlined by thousands of lights, with the ridge of the Chamundi hill in the background picked out by more lights, like Blackpool on a fine summer evening, but somehow, in this setting and clear atmosphere, immensely effective.

For the great European Durbars the Maharaja sat,

graciously impassive, on his throne in the open hall overlooking the courtyard, surrounded by his courtiers, while a dense crowd packed the space below, all mixed up with the State elephants in their best uniforms, the cavalry and infantry in full dress, pikes, lances, pennons and all, the jugglers, acrobats and jesters performing their tricks. The Resident and his staff in uniform drove up in a carriage and pair and passed before the Maharaja, followed by the European guests. This had been going on ever since the defeat of the usurper Tipu Sultan in 1799 and was a way, extended in time, of saying thank you to the people who had given back the property to the old proprietor, even if they had borrowed it again for fifty years.

These were the uneasy days before the outbreak of war. At one of these festivals Dr Schacht was a guest, absenting himself from Germany on an Eastern tour, after a quarrel with Hitler. He did not handle the Mysore ministers very cleverly. One minister explained to him the practical arrangement by which the Government of India kept in their hands the jurisdiction over railway lands in the State territory. Dr Schacht explained, 'Now you understand how we feel about the Danzig corridor', which the minister thought funny. The ministers tried to interest him in a visit to a State factory, but he insisted that he must first go to the post office. They took him there. He would not let the chauffeur post his bulky packet, but posted it himself. He had a touching, if unjustifiable faith in the inviolability of the British mails. So had a German general sent to India by Hitler about this time, in order to observe the collapse of the British Raj. He dined with the Director of Military Intelligence. The D.M.I., General A—, reported the next day, 'I got General von B— drunk last night. He revealed to me ...' General A— also read General von B—'s report home of this incident. He had written, 'I got General A— drunk last night and he told me ...'

We conducted relations between the Paramount Power and the Mysore State, which was not very onerous. We administered the Bangalore cantonment, a little state within a state, with its British garrison and large Anglo-Indian population, through our own courts and police. My duties included persuading the head of the Jesuit Order in the East Indies to get rid of a turbulent Italian priest. The Resident's duties included hearing an appeal from an order of dismissal of a medical compounder for having made up a wrong dose for a high officer. It was a strange coincidence that he had recently suffered severely after an injection, but had been assured by the Residency surgeon that there had been no mistake.

The Mysore Government passionately wanted us to give them back the Bangalore cantonment. The Anglo-Indian community feared that they would lose from it, particularly because their schools in the cantonment were better than the State schools. The army was nervous of letting the State Government loose in their preserves. Someone at the centre, who wanted an easy life, had decreed a compromise designed to satisfy everyone, retrocession with safeguards for all. I learned by painful experience that a decision which is not clear cut never works and that safeguards are generally either ineffective or unnecessary. After years of labour, agreement was obtained on every detail and set out in a document of seven hundred printed pages. It was, I thought, a masterpiece. It was my child and I loved it dearly. I confided it reluctantly to that amorphous and impersonal institution, the Government of India. It sunk without trace. By the end of the war the cantonment had been peacefully given back to the Mysore Government without any safeguards or conditions, when all the questions which had been so hotly contested, were submerged in the great issue of the future of the States themselves.

The Congress party attacked the Mysore Government on lines familiar in British India, organising batches of volunteers to disrupt the administration by 'non-violent' resistance. The police were accused of the standard list of tortures on the party's propaganda list, such as sticking sharp instruments up, fore and aft. The more old-fashioned States handled these volunteers roughly, since they did not have to worry, like the British, about their public image. Even the relatively gentlemanly Mysore police used to adopt what readers of 'Saki' will recognise as the Bertie van Tahn technique, depositing the volunteers miles away in the jungle, from where they would have a good long walk home. They objected vociferously, making up wonderful tales about the dangerous wild beasts which they had encountered.

The State Government was so British in its habits that the ministers were almost as sensitive to political criticism as the authorities in British India. They made a settlement with the local Congress leaders, which was probably quite a sensible way of dealing with the situation, since it saved them from serious trouble until the Congress took over the whole State anyway, when the British left. The only difficulty was how to write the public statement which was to record the settlement without making it look like a complete surrender by the State. The officials tried their hand, but the result was hopeless. Mirza Ismail asked me to help. I heartily agreed with the leader-writer of the *Madras Mail* who, with acute literary judgement, wrote that the statement was a model of its kind. In the Banglalore cantonment we must have been on reasonably good terms with the local Congress, since its leader used to strip to his loin cloth and teach me Yoga exercises before breakfast.

These were the last days of peace of the British Raj, and very agreeable they were. My wife and I had been married in Delhi and spent a week or two in Karwar, where the jungle-covered hills of the west

coast spread down to the sea and where, in sight of
them, lies the little island of Anjidiv, with its seventeenth-century Portuguese church, on which the British
soldiers died of cholera while waiting to take over
Bombay from the Portuguese, who could not believe
that their king could have been so stupid as to give it
away to Charles II as part of Catherine of Braganza's
dowry. There could have been no better life than pre-
war Bangalore for a young couple in the first years of
their married life; a pleasant countryside with an
equable climate, gardens flowering throughout the year,
schooling the horses every morning on the Mysore
Lancers' parade ground, packs of hounds in Bangalore
and Ootacamund, polo and racing, horse shows, big and
small game shooting, visits to the coffee and tea plantations, the antiquities, the ceremonies in Mysore, and
agreeable Indian and British soldiers and civilians meeting naturally in work, sport and the clubs together.
Two of the young Indian soldiers, Kumaramangalam
and Gyani, were to rise to high command in the new
Indian army and kept their British friends throughout
their career; some of the best of the young Englishmen were to die a few years later in Normandy or the
Middle East. I recall too with a vividness born of past
wariness the individual quirks and tricks of the Gunner
horses: no. 7, known as the train because it pulled like
one, no. 9 which reared to the point of falling over
backwards. The docile ones had been appropriated by
the colonel's four daughters.

The Viceroy visited the State. After the visit I conscientiously prepared a volume of ninety-six printed
foolscap pages recording every detail for the benefit of
those who would be organising the future visits of Viceroys which were never to take place. The picture which
stands out in the memory is of the purple, spluttering
face of the Maharaja's stout British private secretary
at the news that the Viceroy's son, now Lord Glen-
devon and his father's biographer, who had arrived a

day early and had caught the fish reserved for his exalted father. The document records:

> The military secretary wrote to say that His Excellency expressed a wish to shoot a bison. The Dewan replied that the Maharaja would be delighted to arrange the shoot, but added that he considered that His Excellency might find it too strenuous, as the programme was full. The military secretary informed the Resident that the Viceroy would not find the programme too strenuous for him and arrangements were accordingly made by the Mysore Government. He shot his bison.

I presume that the State tried to discourage him, since the normal way of shooting bison in those parts is to walk after him for several days until you catch him up. The Viceroy was presumably sublimely unaware that someone must have been sent to round up a bison, shoo him in the right direction and push his nose in front of His Excellency's rifle. It would have been presented to him very differently.

The British army were still not taking life very seriously. I visited a British battalion on exercise. The commander said to me, 'You see that fellow, Major X; he really likes this sort of thing. I would much rather be at home catching butterflies.' In the spring of 1940, just before the German attack on the Western front, I listened to a lecture by a staff officer from headquarters. He said that everything was going splendidly. Even I thought it wildly and irresponsibly optimistic. This halcyon life disappeared for ever with our departure.

We governed the little British province of Coorg, all hill forest of great natural beauty. It rained there steadily for three months of the year, which depressed the planters, who were always in low spirits, being hopelessly in debt on account of the low coffee prices. The

Coorgis, not to be confused with royal dogs, were staunch believers in conspicuous expense. They took their native climate with equanimity and invariably dressed in smart macintoshes. Their estates were all mortgaged to support their ideas of how a gentleman should live. They bred generals of the Indian army after independence and appeared to have nothing in common with the people living round them. They were difficult for the poor foreigner to sort out, since they only had about four surnames and everyone had a different name from his father's. I wrote a superb revenue manual for them, which I hope they are still using. They are a most intelligent and agreeable people, endowed with a happy mixture of courage and improvidence.

In 1970 a Swedish friend visited Mercara, the capital of Coorg. She wrote to me:

Today I have been in your rooms in the Mercara fort. Only the curtained pelmets were left in your vaulted drawing-room. It was transformed into many offices, littered with files. It was Timmi [A. C. Thimmaya, late Indian Chief of Staff] who started talking about you. He showed us some films with the British Raj in all its glory at the races, witnessing the *kheddar*, shooting tigers, greeting Viceroys. I have never had such an acute feeling of post-imperialism as when I stood in front of that fort, so dilapidated, full of corrugated iron, scaffolding poles and debris, trying to become something new. Your office is closed. A Gandhi museum is in the courtyard with a historical section of sorts, containing withered and rat-eaten photos and some copies of documents. In a document of May 7th 1834 I read: 'The inhabitants are hereby assured that they shall not again be subjected to native rule.' The cemetery has been demolished. The little English church was painted yellow. As I entered, I saw men standing on ladders, painting it blue and white. Bamboo poles were lying about. It was very silent. One only heard the strokes of the brush. The stained-glass window was still there. The church is going to be a museum.

I read all the epitaphs, which are to be left. To General Duncan Macpherson, honorary physician to the Queen, and his wife Margaret. 'Blessed are they who die in the Lord.' To Lord Trelawney and his son. To those who died on active service in 1914–1918 and in 1939–1945, from the coffee estates of Ballacadoo Whaddon, Dalquarren, Devarkadoo, Hallery, Huvinikadoo and Kunumbarhulli. To the wife of Sir Richard Burke: 'To live in the hearts of those we love is not to die.'

I was pleased to read in this letter of the Coorgis and their beautiful country and to know that they are using the past and not destroying it, even if they find nothing to create except museums.

From Coorg down the hill it was only a short distance to Malabar, picture-book India, with the teak forests planted a hundred years before by some forgotten Englishman working for generations to come, the warm phosphorescent sea in which we used to bathe at night, the paddy fields and backwaters, the solitary houses not herded together in villages, the unending coconut trees, the bare-breasted beauties, who are probably now fully clothed in deference to the susceptibilities of the new nationalism. This is one of those favoured spots where human beings can live on practically nothing. A couple decide to marry. They drive a few stakes into a backwater. A little island is formed from the silt. They build their house and plant their coconut trees on the island. They fish for food and for money to buy cloth, salt and grain and have found their livelihood.

The Moplahs of Malabar were fanatical Muslims of part-Arab blood. In 1922 they rebelled and murdered and mutilated many Hindus with extreme brutality. During the rebellion, about a hundred and fifty Moplah prisoners were put into cattle trucks ventilated by gratings which had been freshly painted. The British sergeant in charge heard cries at a wayside station, but paid no attention. They were dangerous men and it was not safe to open the door. At the end of the journey they were pulled out, most of them dead from asphyxiation. The member of council responsible wrote on the file, 'This will cause a real ha-ha.' It was the British 'black hole', caused by stupidity and negligence, like the other.

Just over the southern border of the Mysore State were the Biligirirangan hills on the upper slopes of which was the coffee estate of Honnametti. You took an elephant rifle in the car, drove up the hill on a private road, backed round the unfenced hairpin bends and emerged through the coffee plantation on a glorious hilltop looking over a great sweep of forest. The monarch of it all was Ralph Morris, as much at home in the forest as the villagers who lived in it. He was a brilliant shot, tireless, without nerves, liable to fall asleep in the middle of a word or driving on a dangerous hillside, late on the grand scale, not hours, but sometimes days late. Up a tree over a panther kill, he was asleep. The lady guest nudged him, pointing in alarm to something alive sitting above them on a closely adjoining tree, watching them. 'What's that?' she whispered. Ralph woke up. 'Only the panther,' he replied, and fell sound asleep again.

His home was the typical long, low bungalow of the south Indian plantations, littered with elephant tusks, bison horns, tiger heads and skins, and old copies of *Punch* and the *Illustrated London News*. At lunchtime Miyouki, the gibbon, loosed in the forest in the morning, was heard approaching, chuckling to himself with pleasure. There was a rush to shut the windows, or he would swing from horn to horn, drink the ink and

behave like a delinquent child. From there we plunged
into the forest. We lay the whole night on a high platform above a water-hole to watch the game. We slept
on an elephant-track with fires on either side to keep
off the elephants, while leeches fed happily on our
ankles; in the morning we came out of the forest to
see twenty elephants and fifty bison grazing below.
Plunging down into the valley, skirting the elephants,
we tracked bison for days behind the village trackers
who could follow tracks which I could not see at all.

The elephant had been proscribed for killing a man.
He was a single tusker, and had probably become a
rogue from pain in the broken tusk. We slept in the
clearing where he had been grazing the night before;
why, I could not think. I loaded my rifle and woke at
every noise. Ralph was sound asleep in a moment. Next
morning we could not get near the elephant, so the
beaters were sent round with noise bombs to beat him
towards us, while we stood on a rock by the little dry
bed of a stream. He came out at last, a young tusker
guarding him. The excitement was intense. The huge
beast fell at the first shot, got up and plunged off into
the jungle. The young tusker trumpeted with alarm
and crashed away. When it was all over, the villagers
whom he had terrorised came from miles round to see
if he was really dead, the women to gaze on his penis
which would induce fertility. On my return, I picked
up a manual on elephant-shooting. It had a memorable
chapter on the use to be made of the parts of the dead
elephant. The tusks support the gong; the feet hold
the umbrellas; the penis makes an elegant and practical
golf-bag.

It was dawn in the Coorg jungle. The young Coorgi
forester, new to the jungle, walked on ahead. The forest
officer was talking as usual, but at least sober. We were
to meet our two tame elephants to take us to watch the
game. No one had said that the male elephant had been

kept back in the foresters' camp and that the female elephant was on heat. They probably thought it better to say nothing and hope for the best. A solitary tusker loomed up in front. We walked towards him, thinking he was our elephant. He crashed off into the jungle. In the half-light we saw our female elephant on the edge of the clearing and a tusker, this time surely ours, standing by her. We did not see that there was no mahout on her back. He was up a tree. We walked towards them. The tusker raised his trunk and trumpeted, looking at us with extreme distaste for having interrupted him at a pleasurable moment. The young forester raised his arms and shouted, the worst thing he could have done. Our female elephant took fright and ran off. The tusker hesitated between two inviting prospects. We were unarmed. I got ready to run. Though obviously reluctant to give up the pleasure of charging us, he chose the lady and lumbered off after her across the clearing.

They told me in Coorg that an old elephant hunter was on his last shooting expedition in the Coorg hills before retiring to trip over his tiger skins on the floor of an English country cottage. An elephant caught him, took him up in its trunk, broke his rifle and deposited him in a prickly pear bush. Elephants seemed to have a sense of humour and liked to play tricks like overturning the milestones on the main road, which had to be painted black in order to discourage them. At the Viceroy's elephant *kheddah* in Mysore State, the herd driven up the river gave you the same sort of pleasure as the sight of the Horse Guards taking the Queen to open Parliament, but the elephants caught in the stockade were disturbing. One youngster was not in the in-group. The big elephants kept pressing him against the sides of the stockade, trying to hurt him. He was crying out, though I daresay he was not hurt as much as he pretended. It reminded me of my preparatory school.

At one end of the Mysore shooting scale was the tiger-shoot with the Maharaja and the heir. Our position was secure from all risk; rope netting prevented the tiger from getting away; expert shots were disposed around to ensure that the tiger was killed. I hit him, surprisingly in the right place; so did someone else. I was, of course, told the tiger was mine. That meant that I had to have the skin mounted and keep it around until I could decently dispose of what is to me the most awkward and least attractive of house decorations. Five panther skins would at least make a coat for your wife, if she was prepared to bring the jungle into Piccadilly, but I never reached the number required.

At the other end of the scale was a day with the Van Ingens. They displayed their origins and ages by their names, De Wet, Botha, Kruger and Joubert, and mounted the tigers shot by Maharajas and tycoons. You took a gun and a rifle. Perhaps you started with snipe and finished with tiger, dangling your legs over a rough platform hurriedly fixed to a tree eight feet from the ground. Pig-sticking with them meant getting off your horse and advancing on foot with spears at the ready against a wounded boar being bayed by the village dogs, while the ladies retired up a tree.

But what remains in my memory most vividly is spending a night alone in the jungle. The tiger is lurking about, but perhaps is not hungry and does not appear. You settle down in your tree, smeared in mosquito oil. The light fades. The monkeys, the peacocks and all the other birds stop screaming and chattering. Every hour of the night has its own noises, its own distinct quality, until at first light the animals and birds wake up and start their day, like a city waking up with the water carts washing down the streets, the milkmen, the paper boys and the postmen going on their rounds and the men going to work on the early trains.

IO

BAHAWALPUR

T H E temperature was already mounting towards
110°. Hot winds laden with sand blew in from the
desert. I stood in despair while the dust storm raged
outside, my belongings, newly unpacked, littering the
floor and becoming covered with a thick layer of sand
which penetrated the ugly red brick bungalow through
the chinks and gaps in the doors and windows. The old
town was a huddle of mud walls, with slits for windows,
crowded together in narrow streets. In the new town
the public buildings were mean and poorly built, the
officials' bungalows ugly and cheap. There was no
sanitation. A 'sweeper' carried a pail from the house and
dumped the contents over the garden wall into an open
pit. The sun was the purifier. Four months of fierce
dry heat was succeeded by four months of oppressive
humid heat, with always the promise, never the relief,
of rain. I have gone to bed in the garden when the
thermometer showed 96° and woken up in the middle
of the night with it up to 101° and a dust storm getting
up. I have lain in bed on a roof on the edge of the desert
on a still night with no breath of wind, when in ten
minutes a dust storm had rolled up and only my weight
was preventing my bed being hurled off the roof into
the courtyard below.

When in the height of summer we could feel the

sharp heat of the sun but never see it for weeks from the dust in the atmosphere, we sought relief by bathing in the stagnant pool to which the river Sutlej was then reduced after the removal of most of its water for irrigation, sharing the pool with dead buffaloes and cows, but surprisingly coming to no harm. The old villages had the charm of the windowless, high houses of the hot Muslim countries, fortified against the sun and robbers of your wife or gold; the new settlements in the canal 'colonies', as they were called, were wholly without charm. The country was featureless and dead flat, scrub jungle divided into squares of cultivable land, intersected by straight canals. Trees were scarce and, in the new 'colonies', only lately planted, fighting for life against the salt in the soil, the hot winds and neglect.

This was Bahawalpur State, where it was a criminal offence to be seen eating during the fasting month of Ramzan, a desolate tract on the northern edge of the Indian desert, in the hottest part of India, cut from east to west by the Sutlej river, merging into the Panjnad, the five united Punjab rivers, which joined the Indus near the State's western border on the way to Sind and the sea. Its wealth was in its land, irrigated by canals. In the east of the State the council appointed by the Government of India during the Ruler's minority had been too ambitious in designing the Sutlej valley irrigation project. They had wasted large amounts on a network of canals, sluices, rest-houses and roads, which the water did not reach. So the young Nawab had found a huge debt for the repayment of which the State revenues were mortgaged to the Government of India which had been responsible for the mistakes made and now imposed its own officials on the State to collect the revenue and discharge the debt. I was one of them, in charge of the western district which stretched to the Sind border and included the Panjnad 'colony' with an assured supply of water. It was a prosperous area and land was sought there by peasants from throughout the

Punjab. It was also one of the hottest spots in India.

I rarely saw the Nawab, a weak, amiable man who gave little attention to the State and was not often there. When in the State, he lived some miles away from the administrative capital in a palace to which I was never invited. It was the year of the Indian census. The enumerating officer met me near the palace and said, 'Sir, I asked at the palace gate how many women there were inside. Today, after I had waited a week, they told me twelve. What shall I put down?' I said 'twelve'. The Nawab had a habit of keeping prisoners for several years under sentence of death. The other British district officer, who was in charge of the gaol, made a caustic remark in the gaol book, which made the Nawab furious. He was not used to having his actions questioned by officers nominally in his service. We thought it inhuman to keep men in this state of uncertainty for so long. After living in countries in which a sentence of death, earned for being on the losing side, may with luck mean only a year or two in prison, I realise that what is important is to remain alive. The longer you survive, the better chance you have of getting out.

The Nawab had a herd of racing camels which he grazed on the cultivators' fields. We protested and remitted the cultivators' taxes. He must have disliked us very much. Bidden to a ceremonial parade, we were told that the Nawab liked the British officials to wear grey suits and the Indians to wear the fez. My Pathan servant and I both felt the same way about this. I wore a blue suit; he put on his most dashing Pathan head-dress. He was a typical Pathan. Within a week of his coming to me, all the servants were in his debt and in his power. While he was with me, he would have taken any risk to protect me, but he nearly murdered the cook before breakfast and had to leave. Life with him was too tempestuous.

The part of the State administration for which we were not responsible was run in the old Oriental way.

They said that some time before, the Nawab had run out of money in London and had telegraphed for more. The State treasury was empty, but the money had to be found from somewhere. Then some ingenious man remembered that the British Indian post office, which managed the postal services in the State, had a balance of twenty thousand rupees in the State treasury. They took the money out of the treasury and presented it to the post office to pay for a money order of that amount on London. The post office issued the money order and marked up their balance in the State treasury as forty thousand rupees. This was such an easy way of procuring money that they did it four times. The post office found out in due course and indignantly removed their money to the British treasury on the other side of the river. Another revealing story was told me by my Indian assistant. On 1 April the principal magistrate of my district received a telegram signed with the Prime Minister's name ordering him, without giving reasons, to arrest his closest friend, the superintendent of police. The magistrate promptly obeyed the instructions and the superintendent of police had the greatest difficulty in persuading the magistrate that he had sent the telegram as an April fool joke.

The British officials in charge of the two districts could do their revenue work without interference because the State ministers were kept out of it, though they had to collect enormous arrears of revenue in the areas outside the canal 'colonies', left over from the time when the collection of revenue had been in the hands of the ministers. But they had also been given the impossible task of managing the cooperatives and the estates under the Court of Wards, under the State ministers, whose ideas of the financial uses to which these departments might be put were very different from the purposes of the Punjab Acts applied to the State. The British revenue minister, a retired irrigation engineer to whom we were responsible and whom

we regarded as deplorably weak, did not encourage us
to make trouble. I told the Resident for the Punjab
States what was happening, but he chose to do nothing
about it. It was left to his more active successor to clean
the place up.

I rather liked some of the ministers. I realised that
their way of looking at things was not our way and that
it made no sense to judge them as if they were in charge
of the borough council of Chippenham, but this did
not stop us from defeating them whenever we could,
which gave us great pleasure. I did not like the Prime
Minister, who set the tone and was principally to blame
for what was happening. He must often have wished
he could get rid of us. I tore up his order to me to snare
partridges round my district and put them down where
the Viceroy was going to shoot. Perhaps I was being
unnecessarily prickly, but we were not on the same
side. The Viceroy had a very bad shoot, though I suspected that efforts had been made to procure some live
partridges from the Lahore hotels. However, he had
a very good duck-shoot with plenty of birds feeding
happily on rice obligingly provided by the State.

The best of the job was giving land to the hard-
working peasants from the north who could turn fifty
acres of sand-dunes into a prosperous farm in a few
years. We knew that in the long term they would breed
up to their new prosperity and there would then be too
many on the land as in their old homes which they had
left, but we were in an early stage of development of
this area, which had never before been cultivated. We
used the Punjab system by which a man would pay no
revenue or water-rate during the years of reclamation
and would then pay a reasonable price for the land by
instalments over a period of about twenty-five years.
Especially easy terms were given for salty land or where
a condition of the grant was that the cultivator should
grow trees on the edges of the canals. We started a farm
to produce selected cotton and wheat seed. We could

see that what we were doing was helping people; so it was easier to put up with the in-fighting in matters where we had not got a free hand.

We sold small pieces of land by auction. One day about a dozen impressive figures turned up, Baluchi tribesmen, bearded, with immense turbans of tightly twisted cloth, looking like the prophets in the illustrations to a child's Old Testament. For a day and a half they sat patiently, without moving or speaking, waiting their turn, apparently meditating on some deep philosophic concept. We started offering the little pieces of land in the middle of their holdings, for which they were fiercely contending. They promptly lost their heads, crying in dialect, 'Ek to che vi, do to che vi', meaning one over six twenties, two over six twenties, and bid the land, worth about a hundred and twenty rupees an acre, up to seven hundred rupees. I cancelled the sale and started again. This time it was sold for a reasonable price. One could not take advantage of such venerable children. A telegram arrived. I broke off the sale and motored through the night, a hundred miles up the canal bank, another hundred to Lahore. I arrived in the early morning at the hospital. They pointed out the women's wing. There was no one to be seen. I looked in all the rooms until I found the right one. I asked my wife, 'Has the baby come?' 'Yes, a girl.' The Punjab took these little incidents more casually than we do at home.

Maulvi Akhtar Ali, my Assistant Commissioner, helped me to stop the ministers and palace staff getting land meant for peasants by false pretences. He was intensely religious, sturdily independent, with an irrepressible sense of humour and capable of any kind of trick to get his own way. He used to relate with obvious pleasure the complicated manoeuvres by which he had deceived me or other people, but I believed him to be essentially honest and trusted him in the things that mattered, while keeping a wary eye open for his tricks.

I asked him his age. He replied, 'Real age or Government age?' They were four years different. Through him I began to understand the people among whom we were working. It was easy for me to be independent; I had nothing to lose. But his life was in the State and everything he possessed was in it. Yet even if he sometimes cheated a little, I believe that, while he and I worked together, he did what he thought right without thought of his own advantage. It needed courage to resist the pressures put upon him.

Akhtar Ali's father, a retired Punjab official, lived in retirement in the northern Punjab. His son always went to him on leave. In that year, when he reached home, his father said to him, 'I am now going to die. I have made all the arrangements. My grave is ready. Here is a list of neighbours who should be informed of my death and a list of the boys who should carry the news to them on bicycles, with the names allotted to each boy. Here is a list of the people to whom you should send telegrams, with the money for the telegrams. Here is a bag of small change for minor expenses. I always pay your fare to and from Bahawalpur on your leave. Here is the amount.' And so, having detailed the precise arrangements to be made, a day or two later he read his newspaper and died in peace. This is something we cannot do in the West.

I also look back with affection and respect on my 'reader', known as the Mir Sahib. He was infinitely gentle, with a natural dignity of movement and gesture, supremely equable, with a soft but clear voice which he never raised. In Bahawalpur they used the old Urdu office system. A petition was received, written in *shikast*, the cursive Urdu hand which can be so difficult to read. The Mir Sahib wrote a précis of it and of the previous correspondence on the file, in an old-fashioned style, specially kept for official use, replete with Persian and Arabic expressions no longer in current use. This was tied on top of the file, and, as each new development

of the case occurred, a new précis of the file was labor-
iously rewritten. The system had probably not been
changed since Moghul days. For two hours every day
the Mir Sahib sat with me, read me his files in Urdu
and took my orders, which he immediately wrote on the
file. We never exchanged one sentence in English.

In the old cultivated areas much of the land was held
by the hereditary *makhdums*, spiritual leaders who had
acquired large properties from the gifts of their disciples and whose spiritual validity did not seem to be
affected by their personal habits. The largest gathering
of local notables which I saw in the State was at the
wedding of the son of one of the most important *makhdums*. An old-fashioned chief from the borders of
Baluchistan rode in at the head of fifty horsemen, bran-
dishing their swords and carrying their hawks on their
wrists. One *makhdum* present was so holy that the
Ruler used to call on him first, an honour which he
paid to no other of his subjects. My host brought him
to see me in my bedroom, which put me well up in the
social scale. The whole party sat through the night
listening to a famous Punjabi cabaret singer, flicking
banknotes on the floor in front of her as a sign of appreciation. Before the wedding ceremony could begin, we
sat for forty minutes on the floor of a large marquee
waiting for the bride, while the two families argued
about the divorce settlement. This was a matter of
immediate importance since I heard later that the marriage had been arranged against the will of the bridegroom and did not last out the first night.

One day I was in the travellers' bungalow in the
newest and ugliest village on the border of Sind, when
over the desert from Jaisalmer on a camel there rode
in a tiny, neat figure, Sir Aurel Stein, the famous
archaeologist, then nearly eighty. I took him to see the
old sites in the desert on the banks of the Hakra river
bed, abandoned in the middle of the third millennium
B.C., when the river had changed its course and left the

people without water. But the sense of antiquity which he inspired came more from his stories of the old days in Lahore when he and Lockwood Kipling, Rudyard's father, were colleagues. He told me how, one morning after Rudyard had left Lahore, Lockwood Kipling had sent him a note to come over and meet an interesting character who had just come to see him. It was the Tibetan Lama who features in *Kim*. In my copy of Kipling's verse, against the piece beginning 'I go to concert, party, ball ...' is noted in Stein's hand, 'Written by Mrs Fleming, née Miss Kipling', who, as he said, married 'a man in the Commissariat'. This is an archaeological discovery which I believe may not have been recorded. That was another world, somehow seeming more ancient than those old sites in the desert.

I rode round those scorching plains, listening daily to the reports of the Germans' advance on Paris, feeling very much out of the world, consoling myself by reading Gibbon, Macaulay and Motley, trying to help the peasants, if only for my own satisfaction, but knowing that the two systems did not fit together and that the old ways, entrenched for so long, would win, for all our struggles to eradicate them. I was glad to leave.

11

UDAIPUR

A T 4.30 every afternoon the name of God was heard approaching, passing, dying away in the distance, the monosyllable OM, uttered in a deep and resonant voice by a plump and eupeptic priest, dressed in a cloth and the brahmin thread, his body glistening with oil and well-being. I was political agent in Udaipur, ruled by the head of the aristocratic house of Mewar, the acknowledged social leader of the Rajputs. It was one of the most beautiful cities of India. On the edge of the lake the massive white walls of the old palace dominated the town, its little windows elaborately carved with intricate designs. In it was enshrined in sequence the taste of the last three centuries, the Dutch tiles of biblical scenes brought from the trading posts on the west coast to be used as decoration with no thought of their Christian setting, the solid, ugly glass furniture produced by some enterprising English merchant, knowing how to appeal to the oriental love of all that glitters, the little china pots which might have been found over the fireplaces of Brighton boarding-houses, immured for ever in niches in the walls sealed by glass; but, in the main, the simple furnishings remained true to the good Rajput taste – low divans and cushions and white sheets on the floor on which no shoes were allowed to tread. On the island in the middle of the lake was the delicate

little palace, now a hotel, where the British took refuge
in the Mutiny and were protected by the prince, and
seen over the lake was a high fortress rising out of pre-
cipitous rock like a castle in a fairy tale.

The palace ceremonies remained much as they had
been in the seventeenth century. At court the nobles
sat in strict order of precedence, wearing their court
dress of tight turban, divided skirt over tight jodhpur
breeches, and long coat, carrying their curved swords.
In the boat festival, the Maharana sat high on the prow
of a galley that might have been Cleopatra's barge on
the Nile, rowed by banks of oars, while the nobles and
retinue in long white muslin robes grouped themselves
like the chorus in *Aida* on the deck below their
sovereign. For a tiger shoot the Maharana's camp on
the edge of the Jaisamund lake contained stone houses,
hundreds of tents and about a thousand retainers. In
front, the elephants and camels paraded and the skew-
bald horses were exercised in the 'high school'. The
visitor on arrival was taken through an ante-room filled
with courtiers, all in their court dress, into a throne
room where the Maharana sat surrounded by courtiers
of the first rank.

Maharana Bhupal Singh was a cripple, deformed,
shrunk and unable to walk without help. Yet his natural
dignity and presence made his disability appear of little
account. Every afternoon, while he was in Udaipur, he
went for a drive round the town in an open Rolls
Royce, scarlet inside and out, sitting alone on the back
seat, while his aide de camp, himself a noble, squatted
on the floor of the car. Behind were three buses with a
mixed complement of nobles and servants. Every afternoon he stopped at the general store kept by a Parsee
and ordered his entourage to buy some goods, for his
grandfather had promised the owner's grandfather that
if he opened a shop in Udaipur, the Maharana would
give his custom, and the grandson felt obliged as a matter of honour, with the utmost regularity, to fulfil his

grandfather's promise.

Every Tuesday there was a tennis party at our house. The nobles and officials arrived first, clasping their swords and their tennis rackets. The swords were laid aside, the skirts of the court dress were tucked up, and they played remarkably good tennis. A whistle blew; the Maharana was approaching. Tennis stopped in the middle of a rally. Tennis rackets were thrown down, swords were picked up, skirts were untucked and the courtiers stood in line in order of precedence to receive their Maharana. I received him at his car, from which he was helped by two bearded warriors, and walked a quarter of a pace behind him to our seats. I sat on one side of him, my wife on the other. 'May they go on with their game, Your Highness?' I asked. He signified assent. Swords were dropped, skirts were tucked up and the game was resumed. After twenty minutes' conversation the Maharana turned to me and said, 'May I go now?' The whistle was blown, again tennis rackets were dropped, swords were picked up, the procession re-formed and the Maharana walked painfully, supported on either side, between the ranks of courtiers, who made the symbolic gesture of obeisance as he passed. Before getting into his car, the Maharana presented packets of rough tobacco to some of the nobles in attendance, as a token that he no longer required their presence that day. The car moved off and the game was resumed in a more relaxed atmosphere. We introduced one social innovation. My wife held purdah tennis parties for the ladies of the court and Government, all males being banished for the afternoon.

Many of the courtiers still wore the meticulously trained, divided beard, which had been compulsory in the days of Maharana Fateh Singh, who had taken poison to escape from his dilemma at the Delhi Durbar. The Rao of Bedla, the premier noble of the State, had dared to shave off his beard and had been exiled to Ajmer by the old Maharana until he had grown it again. Now he was clean shaven again with the Maharana's permission. This most courtly Rajput noble was an attractive and friendly person. A message came one day, 'Come at once; a panther has fallen into a pit and may be easily shot.' To excuse oneself without being impolite was not easy.

Here seems to be the picture of a State which had got left two centuries behind, a feudal community of nobles, an ossification of old traditions, where it was still a criminal offence to kill a monkey or a peacock, a State living on the traditions of the Ruler's renowned ancestors, whose women threw themselves on the fire in the great fortress of Chitorgarh rather than submit to the embraces of the conquering Muslims. But this was not the true picture. The Maharana was in many ways an up-to-date Ruler, anxious to reform his administration and remarkably liberal in his views. When he succeeded his father, he had astonished everyone by confirming all his father's officers of state in their old positions, instead of making the customary clean sweep. There was a local Congress party called the Praja Mandal (the people's council). The Maharana wisely decided not to ban it, but to register it under the State law and to control its activities. His nobles in Durbar objected. He replied, addressing each one in turn: 'I have arranged for *your* son to be educated at Oxford; I have met the expenses of *your* daughter's wedding; *you* I have helped in your financial difficulties; *your* son I have taken into the State service. What have you ever done for the people? Perhaps the day of the Raj Mandal [the Ruler's council] is past and the day of the Praja Mandal is come.'

For a Rajput the most desirable match for his daughter was the heir to Udaipur. The prize was secured by the famous and formidable figure, the Maharaja of Bikaner, a dominant force in princely politics, host to the aristocracy of Europe for the imperial sand-grouse shoots in his State. He visited Udaipur during that

winter, taking the precaution of peering into a bowl
of oil with copper coins in it, for luck before going out
shooting. Another leading Rajput Ruler came to ask
the Maharana's opinion before marrying a lady from
outside Rajputana. The Maharana replied: 'Whom
you marry is your affair, not mine; but if the Political
Department should ask me whether the son of the
marriage should be treated as in the line of succession,
I should say no.' The little Maharana, in spite of his
crippling disability which prevented him from taking
any part in affairs outside his own State, retained un-
impaired the position which he had inherited as head
of the Rajput clans and used it with humanity and
justice. Though I knew him for only a few months, I
retain great affection and respect for the memory of
this man of old-fashioned habits, who was so dignified
in his bearing, so fine in character and so understanding of the changes which were taking place in his
country.

I became a close friend of his able Prime Minister,
Sir T. Vijayaraghavachariar. We used to discuss local
problems and the inevitable fate of the princely order
which would not compromise with modern ideas and
believed that an obstinate attachment to their
sovereignty in its extreme form would best safeguard
their future. He was a man with a delicious, wayward
sense of humour, who used to say that he liked a slow
train best, because it gave him more for his money. The
education minister, who was later an ambassador
of independent India, conducted one of the most advanced schools in India in this apparently forgotten
corner of Rajputana. These men were making a sincere
attempt to combine a modern administration with the
old traditional relationship of Ruler and people. But
we had no illusions that the experiment would be successful. There was not enough time left.

We lived in a seventeenth-century palace provided
with every comfort and support: marble halls with six

men exclusively employed in cleaning them, fifty prisoners in fetters weeding the terraced lawns and the five perfect grass tennis courts, a hard tennis court for the rainy weather, two swimming pools, a squash court, a stable of horses reserved for us, a carriage for the baby's outings and a guard of fifty soldiers living on the premises. To have refused all this would have given great offence. I used to ride outside the city in the early mornings in the harsh and barren hills rising out of the mist like a Chinese landscape, and liked to sit still, if the under-exercised horse would let me, listening to the distant clanging of the copper-beaters and the other noises of the city in the still, clear air in which every sound was heard. We alone were allowed to stand on the edge of the lake at dusk in that haunting atmosphere of surrounding stillness and distant sounds, while the last light faded behind the improbably romantic castle on the bluff in front of us, and to desecrate the scene with a few shots in the evening flight of the duck. We shot tiger with the Maharana and went pig sticking with the State cavalry. We visited the little States nearby, which were within our charge, one where the Ruler kept albino tigers and black panthers which were apt to get out of their cages and roam round the palace grounds, another where the Ruler was so suspicious of everyone except his private secretary that he invented a secret language known only to the two of them and even issued coinage inscribed in it.

It could have been a perfect life for a time, but we were in the most dangerous period of the war and I could only feel restless in being required to stay out of the stream of great events which were tearing the world apart. I tried to go to the Gulf, but failed. However, I was soon moved to the more active post of political agent in the Bundelkhand Agency in the eastern part of Central India, adjoining the United and Central Provinces of British India.

12

BUNDELKHAND

BUNDELKHAND was the home of the Bundela Rajputs whom the Rajputs of Rajputana considered rather beneath them. One Ruler even organised peacock shoots, which would have been considered in Rajputana to be as bad as shooting a fox in the shires. It had a romantic setting of rocky hills and lakes, dotted with little castles and forts, and fine forests. There was nothing in it that could be called a town. Here the Indian States' system was reduced to its ultimate absurdity. The thirty-three little States in the agency ranged from a State with a population of 360,000 to units of one village with the most primitive administrations. State revenues varied from £90,000 to £1,000 a year. On looking at random through my old notes, I find that State A had been systematically plundered by its Ruler for years. In State B the Ruler spent thirty-five per cent of the revenue on himself and kept an irregular force of gendarmerie to act as beaters for his tiger shoots. In States C and D the Rulers died leaving bankrupt treasuries and large debts. In State E the Ruler was taking for himself over eighty per cent of the revenue. In State F the Ruler had taken sixty-three per cent of the revenue and the whole of the State's reserve, and had removed the account books. And so it went on.

In one month I withdrew the administrative powers from eleven petty Rulers who were not entitled to ask for a commission of inquiry. We started schemes of joint administration which effectively reduced the thirty-three units to seventeen. In the most primitive tract we abolished a still surviving form of serfdom, by which peasants were bound to the service of a landowner, punished for escaping and brought back from the neighbouring States under special extradition agreements. How this state of affairs had survived the eye of so many generations of political agents I could not imagine. We founded a joint agricultural department, a joint teachers' training school and joint armed police reserves. We reformed, as best we could, the police of the tiny States in which the constables were paid only a few rupees a month and eked out their living as farm labourers or by petty peculation. We reorganised the administrations of the States which had come under our control.

The Rulers were a mixed bag. One had sensible ideas about the political future of the States and was looking forward to going into Indian politics. He was diabetic and was ordered by the doctors to play golf. He built a golf course and ordered the State officials to play. All the golfing customs were strictly observed; monthly medal competitions were held regularly; cards were scrupulously maintained. It was an unwritten rule that the Ruler could pick up and place his ball without penalty. Golf was an important part of the State officials' duties, though if the Ruler had given up, every official would have given up on the same day. On the outbreak of war the Ruler had been shrewd enough to realise that the two commodities essential to his life, whisky and golf balls, would become scarce under war conditions. He therefore stocked up with 'Black Label' and Spalding balls and in two years was the only man in the country who had any tolerable brand of either commodity.

In the depths of the jungle a Maharaja said to me, 'I hear that people have been telling you that I am in league with the dacoits [bands of robbers], and that I receive stolen property.' I replied, 'Yes, Your Highness, everyone tells me that.' He denied it, of course, but could have hardly expected me to believe him. He was a cheerful rogue and I had a slight weakness for him after he had accepted with equanimity my proposal that he should disband his army in the interest of economy, a hard decision for him if popular repute was correct in holding that their main task was to provide boys for his pleasure.

The scourge of the countryside was a famous robber, Man Singh, who had terrorised Bundelkhand for twenty years. We formed a special joint police force to chase him. Time and again they were close on his heels, but a judicious combination of violence and charity, in the Robin Hood manner, always enabled him to find out where his pursuers were before they knew where he was. He was finally killed in the middle-fifties, rating two columns in *The Times*. We put a price on the heads of Man Singh and his principal lieutenant. We bagged no. 2 : one night he was shot. I received a detailed report that he had been killed in a fight which he had started, and a photograph of the corpse, his formidable armoury displayed upon his fat stomach and the successful hunters, three villagers, sitting over him with their country-made guns, like big game hunters photographed over a dead tiger. I duly presented the awards in a public gathering. I believed, though I could not prove, that the actual event had been very different from the report. The bandit had been asleep in the village, probably with a girl, and the opportunity was too good for the villagers to miss. They had crept up to him and shot him as he slept, with the muzzle of a gun pressed against his side. He was a murderer many times over. I had perhaps aided and abetted his murder. It was very rough justice indeed, but I could do no more than accept the official version and act on it.

We gave ruling powers to the Maharaja of Chhatarpur, the son of J. R. Ackerley's friend portrayed so vividly in his *Hindoo Holiday*, another book, like Forster's *Hill of Devi*, which reveals the author's attitude towards the Indian Ruler who employed him as a mixture of affection and ridicule. My wife and I were the only British guests at the Maharaja's wedding in one of the temples at Khajraho in his State. On these temples the Chandelas in the eleventh century had portrayed in luxuriant, almost vegetable sculpture, with variety, humour and imagination and with no feeling of obscenity, every possible variation of sexual intercourse, my favourite being the scene where the maid servants are holding the lady upside down by the legs with one hand and suppressing their giggles with the other hand over the mouth. As a Canadian girl remarked, after viewing the sculptures in silence: 'Athletes, I presume.' In those days only the most discreet photographs of Khajraho appeared in books on Indian architecture. Now the temples are a major tourist attraction, photographs of the most involved sexual gymnastics can be bought in the hotels in Delhi and an interlocking prince and his lady are used to advertise Air India.

In Bundelkhand there were some famous examples of seventeenth-century Rajput architecture, notably the palaces at Orchha and Datia. The palace of Man Singh at Orchha is set on the edge of a rocky river. In this setting the old Rulers used to enact the story of the Hindu epic, the Ramayana, over an area of several square miles, with the river representing the strait between India and Lanka (Ceylon), an island in the river serving as Lanka and the rocks between it and the mainland as the bridge made by Hanuman, the monkey god. One part of the building was known by the names of the two hottest months in the Hindu calendar. The

Rajas used to walk in the height of summer in the lower hall, while their retainers in the upper storey sprinkled water through holes in the roof, like a shower bath, to make rain, and rolled great stones up and down the floor to imitate the thunder of the monsoon. Perhaps this performance had an element of sympathetic magic in it.

The palace at Datia was built on a most imaginative design. It was a symmetrical building of seven storeys, each constructed on a different pattern, tapering to the summit and designed to catch every breeze. The grounds of the modern palace were occupied by a wretched zoo, where sad-looking tigers paced up and down their narrow cages, and a guest house where a playful rat had been known to jump on the Resident's pillow at night and scratch him on the cheek.

The Maharaja's main interest was in shooting tigers and he was set on marking up a thousand. One day he wrote to the Maharaja of Gwalior: 'Dear brother, I hear that there is a man-eating tiger causing great trouble to the villagers in your State on my border. I should be most willing, with Your Highness's permission, to rid you of this pest.' The Maharaja of Gwalior, who had no intention of allowing the Maharaja of Datia to shoot it, replied: 'I am most grateful to Your Highness for the information and will speedily myself rid the villagers of this pest.' The wily old Maharaja of Datia was not defeated. He selected a tigress on heat from his zoo and put her in a cage on the border. The Gwalior tiger duly crossed the border to inspect and was shot.

Once more, death seemed to come under human control. In my office in Nowgong was a clerk, an odd little man like a Gogol character, regarded by his fellows with amusement but a certain affection. He had no ambition to rise higher than the humble position which he held, but he lived in continual fear that he might not qualify for his full pension. And so he determined never to take leave, never to be absent from the office for a single day. In the spring of 1943 he told the head clerk that his father would die that summer. He was clearly worried lest the claims of filial piety might conflict with his continuous attendance at work. But he and his father worked it out between them. Late that summer he arrived in the office one Saturday morning with the request that he might leave early at noon, without a day's absence being marked against him, for, he said, his father was going to die that afternoon. The father duly died on schedule. The funeral, attended by all the office staff, took place on Sunday, and the son, having performed his religious duty, was back in office on Monday morning, having succeeded in getting over this crisis without losing a day's work.

We lived in a picturesque bungalow under an immense thatched roof, with a garden swimming in bougain-villaea and paradise fly-catchers nesting in it. Three British officers walked in. The senior officer, a brigadier with a striking gaunt face and piercing blue eyes, introduced himself as Orde Wingate. I knew nothing of him. The impression he made was immediate. We gave him the help he wanted for his training and he disappeared into Burma. During the next summer I told Central Command that our jungles would make a good training area for Burma and that I could promise the cooperation of the States, but they ruled it out. The railway was fifteen miles away to the north and if the train came on time, the odds were that it was a day late. There were two unbridged rivers on the road, to be crossed by ferry. It seemed that they were fighting their war on Salisbury plain. Soon after, we woke up to hear the rumble of army trucks coming through. Wingate had liked our country and house and had decided to use Bundelkhand to train the 70th division, then about to be broken up into long-range columns.

We built him an airstrip. He caught typhoid, and came to convalesce near his troops, staying with us, having told Lord Mountbatten the wholly untrue story that we had a special herd of T.T. cows and all the facilities of a convalescent home. With him came the formidable Sister McGeary, feared by generals and almost able to control Wingate, who swore every day as he set out in his aircraft that he would return that evening, but secretly took his shaving kit in case he did not. Ten thousand British troops moved in. There was hardly an incident between them and the local population – a tribute to both parties. The ladies' jungle canteen was immensely popular. It was astonishing how quickly these young men from the industrial cities adapted themselves to jungle life.

Wingate was an unforgettable figure, Bible in one hand, pith helmet of 1900 vintage in the other, reciting with intensity Emily Brontë's 'No coward soul is mine'; asserting that no civilian was capable of thinking like a soldier, however able in his peacetime profession; relating with a malicious grin how he had displayed the new 'Chindit' flag to the assembled generals in New Delhi and had suddenly realised that it was a lieutenant general's flag, while he was only a major general; taking time off to give rides in his jeep to our small daughter. I stayed with him at his headquarters at Gwalior on the night before he left it for the last time for his campaign in Burma. We walked round the airport in the morning waiting until he could take off. He said, 'Do you know the story of the Italian captain in the first war in the trenches, waiting to attack, with his eyes intent on his wrist-watch? Five seconds, four, three, two, one, zero. Avanti. He leapt out of the trench and immediately fell under a hail of bullets. His men stayed in the trenches, clapping vigorously and crying, "Bravo, il capitano." That is how I feel about this campaign.'

He died in an air accident a month later. Perhaps he was almost looking for death by piling on the risks, from an unconscious fear of returning to the flat life of peace. Some denied the value of his operations behind the

Japanese lines. I am content to rest on the view of an
able and orthodox staff officer of the fourteenth army
who said to me that Wingate invented the technique
of supplying an army by air, which enabled us to win
the Burma campaign.

The war touched us little in Bundelkhand. We received instructions to give ourselves up to the Japanese
if they should reach us, since our primary duty was to
try to protect the civil population, though I could not
see how we should be able to do it while in custody and
thought it more likely that the Japanese would seek to
conciliate the local people. I remember thinking that
it would be a very lonely moment, as the last of our
troops left. But the Japanese reached no further than
the borders of India. We went on with our local affairs,
exhorting, persuading, advising and, when necessary,
acting. If we could make things a little better for a few
poor people, it was enough.

So ended my days as a political agent. George Aberigh
Mackay, whom I have quoted on the Viceroy, described
the political agent as

> a most curious product of the Indian bureaucracy.
> Nothing in all white babudom is so wonderful as
> the political agent. A near relation of the Empress
> some three or four years ago said that he would rather
> get a political agent with Raja, chuprassies and every-
> thing complete, to take home than the unfigured
> 'mum' of Baluchistan. But the political agent cannot
> be taken home. The purple bloom fades in the scorn-
> ful climate of England; the paralytic swagger passes
> into sheer imbecility; the thirteen gun tall talk rever-
> berates in jeering echoes; the chuprassies are only so
> many black men and the Raja is felt to be a joke. The
> political agent cannot live beyond Aden.

Perhaps there was some truth in this in our generation
too. But on this occasion, at any rate, it was not likely

that the aura of the political agent would last even as far as Aden, as my wife and I took two infant children on a four weeks' voyage home through a sea infested with enemy submarines on a ship in the discomfort of wartime, full to bursting with Italian prisoners of war and British soldiers and their families. We were back in the modern world.

13

THE RISE AND FALL OF
THE PRINCES

ANYONE who has read my story up to this point
and who is not familiar with the origins of the British
connection with the States, must wonder how such an
odd situation could have come about and how it is that,
once the British had gone, the princes disappeared so
quickly into the limbo of history. In this chapter I give
a brief account of how I think it happened. This is not
being wise after the event. It is based on a paper which
I wrote in 1943 at the request of the Political Department, in which I forecast with reasonable accuracy
what the structure of India would look like after independence.

When the Indian Empire was in the making, the East
India Company's policy on annexation of territory
varied from time to time and from place to place in
accordance with the practical requirements of each
situation as it arose, with the temperament of the man
on the spot and with the political and financial climate
at home. Conquests came to the British too quickly.
The directors of the East India Company were greedy
for dividends, but not for empire. There were not
nearly enough British administrators to look after the
vast area which was coming under British control. In
many parts of India, therefore, particularly in the first
twenty years of the nineteenth century, when large

tracts of the country were falling to the British power, the policy was to confirm the man in possession at the moment, without inquiring too deeply into his title, if he was prepared to accept a treaty giving him a position subsidiary to the British, in order to obtain the continuation of his rule in a modified form. By this means the officers pacifying a tract could secure the adherence to the British of the people who would otherwise cause trouble.

The process of conquest and decay was arrested and the rapidly changing pattern of a country in a state of anarchy was fixed at one point like a film suddenly stopped in the middle of a scene of violent action. Petty kingdoms which would have lasted only a few weeks were suddenly assured of a permanent future; new kingdoms which had not yet consolidated their territory were pinned to the board in an intermediate stage of conquest; rebellious servants were confirmed in the possession of the booty which they had been fortunate to seize at the right moment, and old dynasties were given a new lease of life at the moment of their extinction. There was no permanent or deep-rooted organisation for the British to recognise. They confirmed the situation which they found as they advanced and so stabilised a chance moment in a period of rapid change. As a result, the territories of many States were inextricably mixed up with each other and with British India, and a map of the States in a political agency often looked like an ink-splash on the wall.

A few examples will illustrate the chequered history of the States. The Mughal Viceroy in Hyderabad made himself finally independent of his master, but remained completely independent for only thirty-six years, threatened by the Marathas in the north and by Mysore in the south. For a brief period he kept his throne by accepting the alliance and consequently the infiltration of the contending British and French and then, for 140 years, a Muslim Ruler of a predominantly Hindu State, remained under the protection of the British. Kashmir was held by a series of Afghan dynasties until the Sikhs gained control. After the first Sikh war, it was ceded in 1846 to the British in composition of the indemnity and was sold by them to a relation of the old Hindu Ruler of the part of the State which lies in the Indian plains, who had risen to a position of importance in the Sikh court. The Ruler was a Hindu, but in the greater part of the State, including its centre, the vale of Kashmir, ninety per cent of the population were Muslims.

The Hindu dynasty of Mysore was old, but it was a puppet dynasty under the heel of a Muslim usurper, being restored to power by the British after they had defeated Tipu Sultan at Seringapatam in 1799. After thirty years of its new existence there was a rebellion against the Ruler, which was the reason or perhaps the excuse for its being taken under British administration. Charles Trevelyan might have succeeded in having it incorporated in the Madras Presidency, if it had not been for his quarrel with the Central Government. In the end, after fifty years of British rule, as I have recorded, it was again restored to the full control of the old dynasty. The most famous and oldest of the Hindu dynasties was the house of Mewar (Udaipur); but this dynasty, which in the person of the great Pertab Singh had resisted the Mughal power for so long and with such heroism, had been reduced by the Marathas in the first two decades of the nineteenth century to the shadow of an independent State and was rescued by the British. Of the smaller States, few had had any title to an independent existence at any period of their history.

The States in their new form were, in a sense, a British creation. They were not a portion of the old India which had remained untouched by British power. Though many could boast a long and distinguished history, for over a century they were an integral part of British rule. They were a reserve of Indian India, with the British patrolling outside the gates. The Rulers were preserved from external attack and internal revolution. The strong Rulers lost their opportunity to carve out new empires from the wreck of the Mughal power and the vitality and force which had made their name feared throughout India. The weak Rulers were saved from a speedy extinction.

The men who carried out the policy of pacification in the States seem to have expected criticism and so presented their system of practical expediency as a doctrine which they called 'indirect rule', while candidly pointing out the advantages to be obtained from it for British interests. While Sir John Malcolm was engaged in pacifying Central India, he took pains to explain in letters written between 1817 and 1821 the changes required in the mode of government, particularly where the new kind of rule was to be tried, which was to control groups of States and preserve them in peace without interfering with their internal administration. He admitted that the Indian Governments were considered to be intolerably bad, but, even if this were true, the contrast of their government with ours would strengthen us. If we made all India into British districts, the dislike of being ruled, common to all men, and the exclusion of Indians from all positions of rank and consequence, which must be the result of our establishing our direct authority, would ensure that our empire would not last fifty years.

Malcolm understood the realities of the power situation better than some British Governments since his day. He argued that we could maintain our power in India so long, but only so long, as we kept our naval superiority in Europe, if we had wisdom enough, which he doubted, not to destroy ourselves by our Indian policy. If that policy required that we should govern a considerable part of India through the Indian princes, we should use all our influence and power to strengthen these 'royal instruments of rule'. Nor should we be diverted from this policy by any considerations of improvement of the States' administration. A policy which allowed the States to atrophy under our overshadowing protection could only be justified if our aim was to take over the direct administration of the whole of India as soon as possible. But this was the great evil against which we had to guard. Territory was coming too fast upon us. We could not prevent accessions of territory and the time might come when the whole country would be under our direct rule; but every consideration required this to be put off as long as possible. We only needed to acquire new territory if it strengthened our power to maintain the general peace, for the prosperity of our own provinces and for the preservation of those whom it was our policy to maintain as Rulers.

Even Malcolm had thought that the British might reluctantly have to annex all the States, as a result of their internal misgovernment. The succeeding generation, which saw the political realities less clearly than Malcolm, tried to expedite the process whenever a Ruler, through maladministration or failure to beget a son, provided a reason for annexation. Blinded by their splendid but complacent vision of an empire which would bring enlightenment to its subjects and honour and glory to themselves, they did their best to justify Malcolm's fear that the British in India would destroy themselves by grabbing too much. The annexation of the State of Oudh helped to bring on the Mutiny. If the princes had felt themselves to be strong, independent Powers, subject only to temporary eclipse at the hands of the foreign invader, the Mutiny was the opportunity for them to become the spearhead of revolt, in the name of the return to the rule of India by its traditional Rulers. Yet so far as they dared, the majority supported the British. The prospect of a safe continuance of their rule, under the protection of a benevolent foreign Power to which many of the Rulers already felt attached by personal loyalty, proved more attractive than the uncertainties of an open competition for absolute power and wider dominion which would follow successful revolution. The British did not ignore the lesson. The doctrine of 'lapse' in the case of a failure of heirs was discarded; deeds of adoption were automatically granted and the Rulers were assured that in no circumstances would their territory be annexed. Even in the absence of a natural or adopted heir, the British selected a new Ruler.

Malcolm's policy was thus revived in a more extreme form than even he had contemplated. Henceforth, the British did their best to avoid interfering in the States' internal administration. Rajas became Maharajas, new titles were granted, gun salutes were increased and the Rulers of the smaller States were elevated from their former subordinate status to that of their more important brethren. The official manual required the political officer to avoid interference unless 'misrule reaches a pitch which violates the elementary laws of civilisation'. This was swinging too far the other way. Protection implied some responsibility for the quality of the regime protected, but the political officers were prevented by this new policy from ensuring a reasonable standard of administration.

In the last half century before independence, developments in Indian communications, industry and commerce made necessary an administrative invasion of the States' internal sovereignty in specific fields in the country's general interests. The States had to allow the British Posts and Telegraphs Department to operate in their territories, if the system was to work on an all-India basis, and to cede civil and criminal jurisdiction over railway lines passing through them, if commerce was not to be hampered and crime was to be suppressed. The States on the western seaboard could not be allowed to divert a substantial share of the Indian customs revenue by developing rival ports and charging cut rates. Difficulties were caused by States attracting industry by the grant of large subsidies or tax exemptions. The negotiations on these points were continuous and complex. The States and British India were getting mixed up.

The Rulers reacted. They paid large sums to British barristers to promote their views. A committee under Sir Harcourt Butler was set up to hear their complaints of the invasion of their sovereignty by the development of the doctrine of paramountcy and the economic requirements of the Government of India; but, after great labour, it produced only the proverbial mouse, that, as was said at the time, paramountcy was paramountcy and could not be defined, and that the economic problems were a tough nut for somebody else to crack. The princes had their trade union, the Chamber of Princes, invented by the British, like the Indian Congress, but it was ineffective. The princes' interests were too disparate. There was no link between a prosperous tract with a harbour on the west coast, a jungle fortress on the Burmese border, a few villages in the Simla hills, the teeming millions of Travancore. The Chamber never came alive.

It will be apparent from the earlier narrative that the political movement in British India did not leave the States untouched. The Congress Party which, with reason, regarded the States as being a part of British rule, attacked the Rulers in the name of the States' people. The Rulers and the Political Department stirred under the impact. The more politically conscious Rulers realised that they must try to put their house in order. Political officers were instructed to 'advise' more often. But this action was irrelevant to the political issue and mutual suspicions between princes and politicians increased. The Rulers feared the effect on their position of the transference of power within British India, which would at the very least entail their relations with the rest of India and the outside world falling into the hands of a Cabinet responsible to an elected

legislature. The Congress Party were not going to leave
the States outside their control.

The Rulers hoped to defend their position by em-
phasising that their constitutional relationship was not
with British India, but with the Crown, so keeping
British India at arms' length. This theory, adopted by
the Butler committee, was the basis of the formal separation of the Political Department from the Government
of India, the creation of a Crown Department under
the Viceroy as Crown Representative to be responsible
for the conduct of relations between the Crown and the
Rulers, and the transfer to the Crown Representative
of relations with those States which had formerly dealt
with the Governors of the neighbouring provinces of
British India. This pattern was reproduced in the proposals for an Indian federation, which emerged from
the series of round table conferences in London. It was
nice and tidy on paper, but all this elaborate effort to
dress up the States' system as something which would
preserve the States as entities separate from the rest
of the new India was doomed to failure. It was a last
effort to swim against the tide.

The princes delayed accepting the federal scheme,
while they argued about the financial provisions affecting them and pressed for constitutional safeguards
against the invasion of their rights by British India.
This was unwise, since the offers made to them were
widely attacked by the Congress politicians as being far
too generous. They had not yet agreed to the scheme
when it was interred on 3 September 1939 with the
uneasy peace. But even if they had accepted it, the final
result would probably not have been very different.
They would never have succeeded in remaining isolated
from British India.

The simple fact was that the British had made sure
that the princes were not able to challenge the British
power and this position was inherited by the successors
of the British in the government of India. The States'

boundaries lay open on all sides; they lay athwart the body of India. The States were widely scattered over the whole country, many of them inextricably mixed up with British India and each other. They could not unite; they could not retire behind their frontiers; they were an integral part of India. All of them were in varying degrees dependent on British India, most for almost everything except grain, and in bad years even for that. Their industry was far behind British Indian industry in its development; their military forces were dependent on the Government of India for their weapons, their training and their supplies, and they could not get military supplies from other sources without the agreement of the Government of India, which controlled the territory round all except a few coastal States. In brief, they had not got the power to stand alone and no one else was going to challenge the Government of India on their behalf, least of all the British who were leaving India on terms of friendship with the inheritors of their power.

Nor would continued separation of the States have made any administrative sense. Both British India and the States had suffered from their administrative separation, and a melancholy tale could be told of schemes for the development of industry, communications and irrigation, postponed for years owing to unresolved disputes between the different governments. Public administration was becoming more complex every year and the old order progressively more obsolete. The majority of the States were so small and backward that they did not deserve a further existence. Moreover, the States' boundaries cut across linguistic and ethnic divisions and it was clear before independence that the new Indian federation would be composed of linguistic units with the States broken up to fit into the new pattern. It was clear too that, if the princes held out against any form of fusion, they would be forced into it. It was not a betrayal of old pledges to recognise the facts and to urge the Rulers to compromise in their own interests.

In the event, the Rulers were completely swept away. The British Government were accused of betraying them when it withdrew the protection of the Crown, which could not be given by any Power not in control of the Government of India. All the efforts of distinguished British lawyers on behalf of the Nizam of Hyderabad were shown to have been irrelevant. He resisted and was duly mopped up. A few princes held titular office for a time as governors of federal units without political power. Many began to take an active part in Indian politics, generally in opposition to the Congress, but their efforts did not suffice to preserve the privileges which had been guaranteed under the constitution. Most public opinion was against them. However, many members of princely families are now working in the home and foreign services. Others are in business. They have a greater opportunity to take a real part in the life of their country than they ever had in the old, securely fenced reserve of Indian India. And now, for better or worse, the political landscape of India is reduced to a dead level plain. Much that was bad has gone, but reformers never pause to think whether what they put in place of the old will be better. With the disappearance of the princes, for all their faults, something has gone which had its roots in the life of India.

14

THE END AND THE
BEGINNING

IN the last days of the war the diplomatic list of the
British Embassy in Washington showed Sir Girja
Shankar Bajpai as one of the nine ministers and me
among the many first secretaries. For all practical purposes we were a separate diplomatic mission, though we
used the British communications system. It was India's
first diplomatic mission abroad, a few years before independence. Most Indian officials in the United States
naturally sympathised with the movement for independence. They were subjected to intensive flattery from
the American 'liberals', which they obviously inhaled
with pleasure, and to the public pressures of Indian
propagandists for the Congress party. It was not an easy
position for them, since American public opinion, inside and outside the Government, saturated with the
old anti-colonial tradition, largely supported the Congress Party against the British Government in spite of
the party's opposition to India's participation in the
war and Subhas Chandra Bhose's connections with the
Japanese. But almost all the Indian officials, whatever
personal connections they might have with leaders of
the Congress or Muslim League, remained loyal to the
Government which they served, although they knew
that that Government would soon disappear and that

they would then be serving the British Government's political opponents.

Bajpai earned the respect of British and Americans during his service in Washington. He conducted himself with dignity and honesty tempered with adroitness. He was abused by his countrymen for it. So was the Indian information secretary who courageously expressed his conviction that India was rightly in the war on the side of the allies. Neither suffered after independence for their loyalty to their service. Bajpai for many years held the post of official head of the Indian Ministry of External Affairs and died as Governor of Bombay. The new Government continued to rely largely on the old Indian officials, knowing that those who had served the old Government well would serve them well.

We were involved in one public controversy, which illustrates the political atmosphere of Washington on Indian affairs at that time. The President's personal representative in Delhi, corresponding to Bajpai in Washington, was Mr Phillips. He wrote to the President a report on the Indian political situation, which became known as the Phillips letter, after it had been leaked to and published by the columnist, Drew Pearson. A member of the State Department told me later that one of his colleagues in the department had given it to Pearson. It created more of a sensation than it was worth, since it said little more than many British in India were then thinking. The Government of India reacted violently and, as we thought, stupidly, by proposing that Mr Phillips should be declared *persona non grata*. Their telegram was addressed to London and repeated to Washington for us, reaching us, as usual, through the British Embassy. This also appeared in Drew Pearson's column. It was difficult to avoid the conclusion that it had been leaked from our office. Bajpai admitted this frankly to the senior minister in the British Embassy, Sir Ronald Campbell, who handled a delicate situation with superb nonchalance. A less sensitive man could have caused great trouble between us.

As the end of the war came near, visitors from India flooded in : a good-will mission, furious at being made to eat at a drug-store on their first evening, the State Department's idea of an introduction to the American way of life; a mission to obtain aid for Bengal famine relief, led inappropriately by a globular politician who had clearly never missed a meal in his life; a Congress politician telling the Americans on his first visit that the British locked up the Indian soldiers' rifles at night, and, on his second visit, when the political climate had changed, that Indian soldiers had played a notable part in defeating the Nazis; the standard visitors always wanting T.V.A., M.I.T. and Parker 51. I was happy working for Bajpai and with my Indian colleagues, but began to feel out of place. I was the last Englishman from the Indian services to take part in representing India abroad.

The Government of India were represented at the Paris Peace Conference in 1946 by rather a mixed group, in which I was an official adviser. The leader of the delegation had made his career under the British and achieved the post of Indian High Commissioner in London. He was out of touch with Indian politics and obviously nervous about his own prospects, especially in the later stages of the conference after Jahawarlal Nehru had taken over the Government. It was very natural, though he did not understand Nehru. He was patently annoyed with the photographers who concentrated their attention on the panache of Sir Khizr Hayat Khan's headdress. Sir Khizr, of the aristocratic Punjabi family of Tiwana, was a man of outstanding personality who was striving desperately against the odds to maintain the unity of the Punjab. He was not going to change his convictions for any political band-wagon, Congress or Muslim League, and had only agreed to come to the conference, under pressure, on the express understanding that he was not expected to take any serious part in it. Sir Joseph Bhore and Sir Raghavan Pillai were two able, senior officials who understood public affairs and took an objective view. The Ministry of Defence was represented first by an amiable British general, who appeared never to have set foot before on the continent of Europe and later by a Pathan who was more at home in tribal forays than in international diplomacy. I represented the Ministry of External Affairs and limited myself to trying to keep the delegation on an even keel. In any case, no Indian interests were directly affected by the outcome of the conference.

When the new Government took over in Delhi, our leader was persuaded erroneously that the best way of earning Nehru's approval would be to vote on the side of the Russians. While I was away for a few days in Berlin, he proposed to Delhi that we should vote for the Russian view on Trieste and received an off-handed consent from Nehru who was probably not interested. A two-thirds majority was required for matters of substance and, as the alignment generally went, the Indian vote on the western side made up the two thirds. The day came for the final vote. Mr Molotov was in the chair. The morning was to be devoted to final speeches by the leaders of the delegations. On the evening before, the Russians told us that our leader was to speak first the next morning. He was not normally in the habit of appearing until the middle of the morning, but on this occasion had to be up early. Mr Molotov, who was obviously impatient with his ponderous interventions, suddenly changed the batting order and put him in last, just before lunch. That was enough for our man. He retired after lunch and handed over the job of voting on the Trieste issue to Sir Joseph Bhore. Our leader would have undoubtedly voted for the Russians, who would have secured their aim to defeat the Trieste statute. Sir Joseph paid no attention to the instructions from Delhi and voted solidly all the way through for the Western side. So the Trieste statute came into existence and Mr Molotov defeated himself.

There was another near shave on the Danube issue. In the uncertain Indian political atmosphere it was obviously good tactics for me to encourage our delegation to vote against the British on some minor matters, which would satisfy them that they were being independent and would make it easier for them to vote with the British on the important issues. I was not being disloyal to Indian interests. Nehru had not yet produced his new foreign policy of non-alignment and we were still on the old tack of general alignment with British views on matters of no importance to Indian interests. So one day we voted against the British. Alexander, then deputising for Ernest Bevin, looked up angrily at our delegation. I knew what trouble that look would cause. It was bitterly resented and I sympathised with the Indian reaction. The British delegation understood and, at my request, Alexander went out of his way to be friendly to the Indians. But that glance still rankled and in that atmosphere it looked as if the crucial Indian vote would be lost this time. I argued hard with Pillai, but he had convinced himself that the Communists were right on this question. I gave up and went to bed. Next day, I learned to my surprise that the Danube statute had been just passed with the aid of the Indian vote. Pillai had changed his view at the last moment after the Chinese nationalists, who were then close to the Indians, had voted for the Western view.

I had learned that chance plays its part in international conferences. Later, I reflected that neither of these decisions had any effect on the international scene, since power settled these disputes in the end, as usual. It was a long and wearisome conference. It provided me with the only occasion on which I have felt active sympathy for Mr Molotov, when he remarked testily that Dr Evatt's manifold amendments to the

Italian treaty, which had highly embarrassed his own delegation, were wholly out of proportion to Australia's interests in the matter. The conference had been made tolerable for me by my personal friendship with three Indians, who were the equal in ability and character of anyone at that conference – Khizr Hayat Khan, Joseph Bhore and Raghavan Pillai. I knew that India, with such men at its disposal, would be well represented in the international field. For many years I kept in touch with Sir Khizr Hayat Khan, who had maintained his views to his own disadvantage during the first years of Pakistan's existence and was still insisting, as late as 1969, that the British Government had betrayed their promises to him.

I returned to India to work for Jawaharlal Nehru. It was a stimulating experience. Here was a man who had spent his life fighting the British, who had only recently been released from prison, but who appeared to be completely without bitterness. He seemed to assume that the British working for him would think only of Indian interests and so he had our loyalty. He made no move to 'indianise' the department, which was still almost completely British. We took the initiative. He treated questions of external relations objectively, did not overrule his officials for political reasons, whatever he might say in his speeches outside the office, and was always ready to reconsider his decision, if we showed him that there were valid objections to it.

Nehru was not objective when dealing with frontier affairs, with which I was not personally concerned, but for him they were a matter of internal politics, part of his fight against Jinnah. He lost his composure when dealing with the Pakistanis. Some time after the announcement of partition, it was decided that the Pakistanis should be given the opportunity to form a foreign ministry in embryo from a nucleus in the External Affairs Department. Mr Ikramullah, later Pakistan's High Commissioner in London, was nominated as the first head of the Pakistani department and we were to find him a room. I offered to give up mine, two doors away from Nehru's room. Nehru insisted that he should go downstairs where the junior officers and clerks had their offices. Ikramullah refused and threatened to pitch a tent on the lawn outside. Nehru gave way, though with bad grace. Ikramullah was a man of resource. He once said to me in London, 'You know all those letters which have been appearing in the press about Kashmir from retired British officers? I write them.'

We were soon engaged, in what the Pakistanis called the Hindu affairs department, in establishing India's new foreign service and ministry on a sound basis. Bajpai had now returned to India, having been met at the airport only by members of his family, one old friend and me. I was not surprised when, a few weeks later, he appeared in the department as Nehru's adviser on foreign affairs. Nehru recognised his qualities and experience and he quickly became secretary general, a name which he made me pick from a choice of three as the designation of the official head of the department, characteristically leaving me in no doubt which he preferred. I wrote three memoranda for Nehru containing recommendations for training and recruitment, a programme for the establishment of diplomatic relations with other countries, and a plan for the organisation of the Foreign Ministry. Recruitment was started, diplomatic missions were opened and administrative rules were drafted. I look back with real pleasure at the small part I played in starting to build the Indian Foreign Service and was genuinely pleased when, many years later, a senior member of the service who accompanied Prime Minister Shastri to Moscow told me that they still regarded me as a member of it.

Nehru was at his best during these years. When he propounded his policy of non-alignment, I thought it too negative a concept, which could not be maintained for very long. Those were the days when it was assumed that the newly independent countries of our old empire would automatically align themselves with us against the Communists. We have moved a long way since. The Indians' mistake during those early days was to adopt an attitude of moral superiority in foreign affairs, which annoyed everyone else and could hardly be sustained when the issues of Kashmir, Goa and the Indian-Chinese borders showed that the Indians were no better than the rest of us when their own interests were involved.

The time had now come for the British officials to think of their own future. We could have stayed until we had earned a full pension, but were given no special encouragement to do so. We did not resent this; we thought it right that the many able Indians in the services should replace us. Nehru asked me to stay on for a few months after independence, but I felt I should not do so, since I had to start a new career. Nehru wrote on the file, 'I will not stand in his way, but I am sorry to see him go.' It was a good note on which to end my Indian service. I met Nehru several times afterwards and he always showed me the same friendship as he had during these few months when I worked for him. For the same reason I refused an offer from Pakistan. I left India two weeks before independence and the terrible tragedy which swept over the northern plains during the first few months' existence of the two newly created States.

The days of struggle against the British had been an exhilarating time for the Congress politician. The great issue of independence dominated and simplified politics and excluded all internal differences save communal strife. It was exciting and stimulating to defy the Government and be sent to prison, thus simultaneously acquiring merit as a self-sacrificing patriot and advancing one's political career. Tedious problems of administration and inconvenient responsibilities were for the future. Besides, there was no doubt who would win and surely virtue would not have to be its own reward.

There were visions of honour and comfort as governor or ambassador. In some ways independence must have been a disappointment. The excitement of rebellion was gone and was replaced by the prosaic business of running the country, keeping law and order and dealing with the same old intractable problems in much the same way. The real disaster for a revolution is to be successful.

By power imposed from the outside we had given India unity, one of the main benefits conferred by British rule. What would have been the fate of the sub-continent if the British had never been there or had not advanced beyond the trading ports? Perhaps the Russians would have reached the Indus, there to be stopped by the power of the Sikhs. Ranjit Singh would have disputed the lordship of Delhi with Holkar and Scindia, the Maratha chiefs. Bengal would have been an independent kingdom engaged in continual strife with its neighbours. The remains of Mughal power at Hyderabad and separate Dravidian States would have contested the dominion of the south. The game of speculation on what history might have been is endless.

We failed to leave India in unity, but in this crisis of affairs there was no solution except partition. The knot had to be cut. When the first terrible pains of partition were overcome, the old prophecies that we should be succeeded by chaos, not a rupee or a virgin left, which few of us in India had believed, were proved false. Two armies were made from one; the princes lost their powers and their States were swallowed up; but apart from the dislocations and personal distress resulting from partition and the disturbing enmity of the two new States, life in most of India went on much as before. The last British Viceroy became the first Governor-General of independent India and left with demonstrations of Indian affection, though inevitably with distrust from Pakistan. British officers visiting their old regi-

ments found the old traditions and customs maintained
by their successors, known in India as the 'brown sahibs',
and the portraits of the old British commanders still on
the walls of the mess. British firms increased their stake
in both countries and there were for a time more British
civilians there than in the old days. The British people
were well disposed towards the new countries and gave
them generous economic aid. There was no bitterness
in the minds of Indians or Pakistanis about the past. In
spite of all the years of political struggle, Charles
Trevelyan's forecast of the way in which independence
would come about was in the main fulfilled.

So ended British rule in India. For a hundred years
and more the country had been ruled by the sons of the
English country rectory or of those family dynasties
which traditionally made their lives in India. We of
the last generation served India to the best of our ability,
without any missionary spirit or feeling of dedication
or devotion to a cause. We served because it was our
job and because we enjoyed it. Our Indian friends
seemed to consider us sympathetic without being
patronising. We had little use for Englishmen who
ceased to be English and tried, from the best of motives,
to become Indian in outlook and habits. We believed
we could best serve our own country and India by remaining ourselves. When Indian and British interests
conflicted, we took the view which we thought right for
India. We were convinced that the British had brought
great benefits to India, but, in the end, that it was time
for us to leave. India was our life. That life was, in
part, harsh and unattractive and cut us off from our
own country, but it was, in the main, rewarding. We
were content that we had chosen it.

Now twenty-five years have passed. New attitudes
and alignments have taken shape. The imprint of the
British past is less strong, but will never be wholly
obliterated. The problems of both India and Pakistan
are insistent and troublesome. There have been errors

and achievements. The tragedy of the migration through the Punjab has been succeeded by the tragedy of the migration from East Bengal, the fourteen days' war that followed and the creation of Bangla Desh. In the course of this upheaval there has been terrible suffering. None of us can have been surprised that the two so widely separated parts of Pakistan have failed to keep together. Perhaps neither India nor Pakistan has yet found its new identity. For mc this is symbolised by the empty canopy at the bottom of the great processional way in Delhi. King George V has been politely removed. At the time when I write this, no one has taken his place.

INDEX